K9 MEDIC

How to Save Your Dog's Life During an Emergency

Eric "Odie" Roth

TWO HARBORS PRESS

Copyright © 2013 by Eric "Odie" Roth

Two Harbors Press
322 First Avenue N, 5th floor
Minneapolis, MN 55401
612.455.2293
www.TwoHarborsPress.com

All rights reserved. No part of this publication may be reproduced, stored in a retrieval system, or transmitted, in any form or by any means, electronic, mechanical, photocopying, recording, or otherwise, without the prior written permission of the author.

The publisher and the author make no representations or warranties with respect to the accuracy or completeness of the contents of this work and specifically disclaim all warranties, including without limitation warranties of fitness for a particular purpose. No warranty may be created or extended by sales or promotional materials. The advice and strategies contained herein may not be suitable for every situation. This work is sold with the understanding that the publisher is not engaged in rendering legal, accounting, or other professional services. If professional assistance is required, the services of a competent professional person should be sought. Neither the publisher nor the author shall be liable for damages arising here from.

ISBN-13: 978-1-62652-404-0
LCCN: 013916873

Special thanks to photographer Julie Powell.

Distributed by Itasca Books

Printed in the United States of America

This book is dedicated to my family, who allow me to spend countless hours teaching and sharing my knowledge. Also to the people who love their dog as a family member, and to the people dedicated to the care and well-being of all dogs, both large and small.

CONTENTS

Foreword ix

Introduction xv

Chapter 1 1
First-Aid Kits

Chapter 2 7
What's Normal?

Chapter 3 16
Approaching an Injured Dog

Chapter 4 19
Restraining and Muzzling an Injured Dog

Chapter 5 30
Artificial Respiration, Chest Compressions and CPR

Chapter 6 45
Choking

Chapter 7 53
Shock

Chapter 8 58
Injuries and Bleeding

Chapter 9 80
Pad Wounds

Chapter 10..83
Seizures

Chapter 11..91
Sprains, Strains, Fractures and Dislocations

Chapter 12..98
Bloat

Chapter 13..108
Poisons

Chapter 14..116
Heat Stroke and Frostbite

Chapter 15..121
Administering Medications

Chapter 16..125
Other Injuries and Illnesses

Chapter 17..140
Disaster Planning

Chapter 18..147
Saying Goodbye

Chapter 19..151
Conclusion

Index..155

About the Author...165

FOREWORD

In early 2009, I bought some human CPR mannequins for my CPR and AED training business. That's when I saw a canine mannequin for sale. My first thought was that this equipment must be for veterinary schools or hospitals. Curious, I went onto a popular search engine and typed in "dog CPR." I was surprised at the results—or should I say the lack thereof. I found little information on how to perform this life-saving maneuver. I then typed in "dog first aid." I found articles on certain subjects; however, there was no one place to learn how to perform basic first aid for dogs.

I once read that there are over 74 million dogs in U.S. households. So why is there so little information available regarding how to care for them in the event of an emergency? In his book *A Member of the Family*, Cesar Millan mentions "on the importance of knowing what to do in the event of an emergency and the importance of having a first-aid kit." I thought to myself, "With as many dog owners as there are, this information needs to be accessible." Sadly, I was not able to find such a class in my hometown of Denver, Colorado. That's when I thought, "Who better to learn life-saving skills, first aid, and CPR from than a paramedic?" Having been a dog lover my entire life, I had found my new mission.

I have been teaching a paramedic version of canine First aid and CPR since 2009. I have taught this vital information to thousands of dog lovers since that time. With social media evolving I started to field calls from dog owners in other states who wanted me to teach at their location. Needless to say it just wasn't feasible for me at that time. And that is how this book came to life. I hope you find the information clear and concise, as I attempted to write it in what I call normal language. I hope reading it gives you a better understanding of what to do in the event something happens to your dog. Lastly, I hope this book will provide you with the confidence to perform first aid. I hope you will be able to worry less with the knowledge that you will know what to do should something go wrong. When dogs are injured or sick, I often hear their owners blaming themselves because they couldn't do more, or just did not know what to do. Learning the information presented in this book will help prevent that situation. In addition to this book we are working on a K9 App that will encompass this information as well as a online training academy.

How I Started Saving Canine Lives

I was a paramedic working twenty-four-hour shifts and trying to juggle the busy life of a father and husband while also attending online classes. My human CPR business was also getting busy; I was teaching CPR at doctor and dentist offices, kidney centers, children day care facilities, fitness centers, and wherever else people wanted to learn CPR. Now I also found I had a demand for pet owners wanting me to hold canine CPR and first-aid classes. I asked myself how I could find the time for that. I wondered if I should commit myself to this new direction even though I was already burning the candle at both ends. Then I received an email from one of my dearest customers, Angel Service Dogs.

To do this book justice, I must first introduce you to Riley. Riley is a child who has a life-threatening peanut allergy. She also had a service dog named Rock'o. Rock'o was trained to sense the presence of peanuts and alert Riley before she was accidentally exposed to a peanut, or even a particle of the protein in the air. The dog allowed Riley to live a normal life without fear of becoming gravely ill or dying due to her peanut allergy.

Rock'o had such a positive impact on Riley's life that her family created Angel Service Dogs. The program trains service dogs for children with life-threatening allergies and raises money to offset the cost to families. I started working with Angel Service Dogs a year before I received this letter, which partially inspired me to write this book:

Odie,

We had one of the dogs in training at our house today and a very freak accident happened. I heard Riley screaming outside. I looked outside, where she was giving Rock'o and Artie a bath in our outdoor wading pool (like the one we used at the parade). Artie had caught his leg on the underside of the plastic pool. The plastic had caught his leg, cut an artery, and cut to the bone (seriously, didn't know this could happen). Riley had grabbed her pack, put gauze as a muzzle on his mouth, took another gauze pack and put it on the wound, and taped vet wrap around it to hold it and stop the squirting when his heart beat. She then tells me, I checked his pulse and he seems to be OK, we need to get him to a vet. We had him to the vet inside of twenty minutes. When the vet took the wrap off, it started squirting again. The vet was impressed with the wrap, to which Riley said, "I learned it in K9 CPR class."

  He is now recouping in his crate. We think his leg will only have minor nerve damage. Time will tell. We are estimating he lost a pint of blood, which most certainly would have been more.

  So Thank YOU.

Sherry Mers
AngelServiceDogs.com

After reading this email, everything became clear to me. My newfound mission was making a measurable difference. One of the local news channels picked up the story and put together a heartwarming segment about it. In closing, Sherry told the reporter, "When you look at the full circle of what happened, where you have a little girl who relies on a dog to save her life every day, and then when a dog was in danger, she saved that dog's life, and now that dog is going to go on to save another little girl's life—that's just incredible."

Without Riley's actions to control the bleeding, there is no doubt in my mind that Artie would not have made it to the vet. I had successfully trained a ten-year-old child to save a life. This goes right along with my unofficial company motto: "Since there's no 911 for dogs, I just try to close the gap."

Artie was able to go on to graduate from the Angel Service Dogs program, and went to work protecting a little girl in Alabama—all because Riley knew what to do to save his life.

INTRODUCTION

Working as a paramedic for a busy 911 system, I have seen many things, including childbirth, shootings, stabbings, deadly car accidents, falls, assaults, suicides, strokes, heart attacks, seizures, and many other emergencies. You are reading this because you care deeply for your dog and want the very best for them in the event of an emergency. French microbiologist Louis Pasteur once said, "Chance favors only the prepared mind." This is especially true when it comes to first aid. I will teach you how to take care of your dog as a paramedic would a human.

    I can't speak for everyone, but when I think of the whole concept of having a dog, I think about all the ways that dogs help human beings. They track people trapped by avalanches. They search for missing people in the rubble of disasters. They save drowning people, and have been known to take a snake bite for a toddler. They pulled our loads in the past, and have put food on our tables. They have tended our flocks and protected our homes. They put smiles on our faces and bring happiness to those in the hospital or a nursing home. They serve as arms and legs for the paralyzed. They lead the blind. They can warn an epileptic when they are about to experience a seizure. They find our lost children and escaped convicts. They find bombs, drugs, and even peanuts for those with severe allergies. They can also smell cancer.

Most pet owners agree that companionship—love, company, and affection—are the greatest benefits to adopting a dog. Fifty-nine percent of pet owners say pets are good for their health and the health of their family, and that their dogs help them relax. Most of them let their dogs sleep in their beds. Forty percent say that owning a dog motivates them to exercise on a regular basis.

Most of all, our dogs are our constant companions. They offer us unconditional love. They don't care what kind of car you drive, what kind of job you have, what kind of house you live in, what kind of clothes you wear, how much money you make, what color you are, what you look like, or even what you smell like.

I sometimes joke with my wife by asking her if I were to put both her and our dog, Buddy, in the trunk of a car and leave them for five minutes, who would be more happy to see me when I let them out? I'm sure Buddy would be wagging his tail frantically and wanting to lick me. The response from my wife would certainly not be as pleasant. Of course this is a joke, but it is just an example of the level of unconditional love dogs give us. It's no wonder that from time to time I hear the phrase, "The more people I meet, the more I like my dog!"

With that said, I feel that we have not done dogs justice. Yes, we spend millions of dollars on food, vet bills, obedience training, toys, and more. But how many dollars are set aside for actually taking care of your pet in the event that they get hurt? How many people would know what to do in the case of an emergency? How many people have attended classes to learn about these subjects? These were among the many reasons that I wrote this book.

Those that are involved in the medical field know how much effort and education is involved in obtaining medical degrees and keeping certifications current. I feel there is a huge void in the same areas for pet treatment, and I believe that I can fill that void.

First Things First
When learning to care for a dog in an emergency, the first thing you must learn is how to maintain your own safety. Never under any circumstances perform any procedures if you are not safe yourself. If conditions are not safe, you must first make them safe before proceeding.

Do you ever wonder why fire trucks block all three lanes of traffic when there is a minor crash on a highway? It's so the traffic does not take out the medic. Paramedics obviously cannot provide care to the injured if they are injured themselves. Fire fighters are trained to make every situation the safest it can be prior to performing any type of care. When I am called to a shooting, I stay blocks away from the scene until the police have determined that it is safe for me to be there. The fact is that you will be unable to provide care if you are injured or dead. Take the time to make the scene safe. Your safety is of the utmost importance.

I want you to think like a medic. When reading this book, keep in mind that I am not a veterinarian, I am a "Paramedic" who feels that there is a void in providing emergency care to pets prior to reaching the veterinarian. Many of the same paramedic skills that are used to save humans can be applied to our dogs. That is why the majority of the topics covered in this book deal specifically with how to recognize and treat injuries prior to taking your dog to receive professional veterinary care.

I once had a woman ask me, "What makes you think you're qualified to teach this?" I told her that if you want to learn how to bake a cake, you go to a baker. If you want to learn how to perform life-saving procedures and first aid, you go to a paramedic. I then told her that if she took my class and was not satisfied with the content, I would refund her money. Well, during the first break she approached me and stated she would not be asking for her money back. All people need is the training and desire to help to make a difference. You might be familiar with Dr Henry Heimlich's technique for dislodging food or objects caught in people's throats. Dr Heimlich has been credited with saving untold thousands of lives around the world since he invented it in 1974. At the young age of 96 years old he performed his technique for the first time saving the life of a woman in a nursing home. The bottom line is that I am a paramedic and I can teach you how to do deal with emergency situations as a paramedic would.

The information in this book is not intended to take the place of your veterinarian, as he or she plays a crucial role in the care and well-being of your pet. When I have someone in the back of my ambulance suffering from a heart attack, I try to stabilize the person, but I also take the patient to the hospital, where he or she can receive care from trained professionals with the resources to provide the best care possible. We must keep the same principles in mind in emergency situations involving dogs.

Although this book will provide you with the basic knowledge to handle many emergencies, it is important to bear in mind that dogs of different sizes must be treated differently. And just as in human medicine, there is controversy regarding how best to handle certain situations. There are some situations in which I would strongly encourage you to do additional research before determining your best course of action. One example of this is bloat. Bloat is a condition that can be fatal to your dog within one hour if not identified and treated. When it comes to bloat prevention, some experts believe it is best to elevate food bowls when feeding. Others feel this does not provide any benefit and may even increase the risk. Who is right? You must make that decision for yourself and your pet based on your feelings after looking at both sides and talking with other people familiar with your breed of dog. The purpose of this book is not to answer questions such as these, but rather to educate dog owners regarding the signs and symptoms of bloat and what important steps you can take to save your dog once you have identified the emergency.

The term *emergency first aid* refers to actions you can take within the first few moments after an event. You can safely use your newfound knowledge to stabilize your dog before transporting him to the veterinarian. It is important for you to be prepared and ready to handle any type of emergency.

You may need to read this book several times before you feel confident that you can perform the procedures necessary to stabilize an injured animal. This book is not intended as a quick reference guide. Would a paramedic look at a "how to" book prior to splinting a broken leg or running a defibrillator?

It was also not my intention to write a "doom and gloom" book. Please know that in each discussion, I have attempted to paint the worst-case scenario. Often paramedics think two and three steps beyond what is currently happening, hoping for a favorable outcome. That is why we train and prepare for the worst-case scenario. I believe being able to save a life is one of the most rewarding feelings anyone can experience. Feeling helpless is one of the worst. truly hope that **K9 Medic** will strengthen your knowledge about providing first aid to your beloved dog and will eliminate the feeling of helplessness. I know people who have lived with a lifetime of guilt because of a tragic event during which they feel they could have or should have done more. Hopefully this book will give you the knowledge you need so that if an accident does befall your dog, you will be able to do everything in your power to help.

CHAPTER 1
FIRST-AID KITS

Do you know where your nearest twenty-four-hour animal clinic is? You should.

Imagine you are in an ambulance having a heart attack and you notice the EMT driving is looking up the hospital's address to figure out how to get there. EMTs obviously need to know where the nearest hospital is. The same applies to your dog's medical care providers. Do not wait until you have an emergency to find out where to go or who to call. Take the time to do the following:

1. Put the closest twenty-four-hour animal hospital's phone number in your phone. Place it on speed dial or write it down

and keep it in your first-aid kit.
2. Know how to get there. If you need to practice a good route, do so.
3. Have a plan. If you live alone or have a large dog, you may need help to get her into your car or truck when injured. Ask a neighbor if they would be willing to help you, if necessary, in the event of an emergency.
4. When planning to travel, take the time to find out the locations of the animal hospitals in the area you plan to visit.
5. There are also several mobile phone apps now on the market that will allow you to find the nearest animal hospital.

By having this information on hand, you will be able to give your dog your attention and avoid the stress of having to look up information during an emergency. If you are faced with a life-or-death situation, the chances your dog will survive will improve greatly if you are able to reach a veterinary hospital within twenty minutes.

First-Aid Kits
It is important to create a first-aid kit specifically for your dog. Without a first-aid kit, you are nothing more than a well-educated bystander.

Imagine for a moment that you have a sudden occurrence of chest pain, as well as feeling a bit weak and nauseous. You're afraid you might be experiencing a heart attack. You are alone, so you call your emergency services number (which is 911 in most areas). A few minutes later, some guy shows up at your door with his hands in his pockets, with no ambulance, no high-tech equipment, and carrying nothing. How confidant would you be in his ability to save your life? Or let's say you take your car to the mechanic for some engine repairs. He then has you pull into an empty garage and tells you he will call you

FIRST-AID KITS

when it's done. You get the idea. Why do we as a nation put so much emphasis on medical equipment? Because without it, chances for a positive outcome are extremely slim.

As a paramedic, when I report for duty in the morning, the first thing I do is check my equipment to ensure that it is operational and that I have enough supplies for any kind of situation. The Boy Scout's motto, "Be prepared," is never truer than when it comes to emergencies. You must have a first-aid kit.

If you are an active person who enjoys hiking and other outdoor activities with your dog, I would recommend that you have a second kit to take with you during outside activities.

There are many preassembled first-aid kits available for purchase, or you can build your own. I personally like to build my own kit for several reasons. First, it can be less expensive, since you can find many of the necessary items at your local pharmacy. Second, building your own kit allows you to include only the items that you feel are necessary. Keep in mind, building a first-aid kit for a Jack Russell terrier

K9 MEDIC

will be quite different from creating one for a Great Dane. For large dog breeds, you will need larger medicine syringes and more supplies, such as splinting and bandaging materials. If your pet has special medical conditions, you will need to ask your veterinarian what additional items you should include in your kit.

Check your kit periodically and replace expired medicines. It is also a good practice to replace items as soon as possible after using them so that your kit is always ready to use.

Your pet first-aid kit can be stored in a small, sturdy box. Be sure to keep your kit (and all medical supplies) out of the reach of young children and pets.

First-Aid Materials
- Absorbent compresses (sometimes called gauze sponges) in assorted sizes. These are good for controlling bleeding.
- Adhesive tape in both one-inch and two-inch widths.
- Antibiotic ointment for use on scrapes and cuts.
- Blanket. These can be used to carry an injured dog, among other uses.
- Coflex (aka Vet Wrap) this will be used for many things including bleeding control and splinting.
- Cold compress. These are used to treat sprains, strains, and broken bones.
- Diphenhydramine (Benadryl®). This medication is used to treat allergic reactions. The dosage will depend on your dog's weight (one to two milligrams per pound). The maximum dose is fifty milligrams. This medication has an expiration date and will therefore need to be replaced from time to time.
- Expired credit card. This is used to scrape away insect stingers.
- Gas-X strips. These are useful for treating a dog with bloat.

FIRST-AID KITS

- Gloves, disposable and nonlatex.
- Glucose paste or honey packets. You should include these in your kit if your pet is diabetic or has a history of low blood sugar.
- Hydrogen peroxide, 3 percent. This is used to induce vomiting. Dosage is weight-based, approximately one teaspoon per ten pounds of dog. The maximum dosage is nine teaspoons. It's a good idea not to give this medication until you are in the location where you want your dog to vomit, as the reaction will be swift. Be sure to check the expiration date on this product from time to time.
- Kerlix, two rolls. This is used to control bleeding, to treat burns, for splinting, and several other purposes.
- List of emergency telephone numbers, including your after-hours emergency veterinary hospital and the Poison Control Center (1-888-426-4435).
- Muzzle. Kerlix can also be used to make a temporary muzzle.
- Nail clippers, appropriate for your dog's nails.
- Needle-nose pliers.
- Nylon leash.
- Penlight.
- Non Petroleum jelly.
- Plastic bag. These can be used to collect samples, if necessary.
- Rectal thermometer, nonmercury/nonglass. It might be a good idea to mark *DOG* on it as well.
- Scissors. Make sure they have blunt ends so you do not accidentally poke the dog, which could cause a puncture wound.
- Sterile eye lubricant (available at pharmacies)
- Sterile gauze pads, nonadherent, assorted sizes
- Sterile saline eyewash (available at pharmacies). This is used

to wash foreign objects such as grass seed from the dog's eyes.
- Sterile, water-based lubricant (such as KY° Jelly) that washes off easily. This can be used to keep the dog's fur away from wounds during treatment.
- Stethoscope. This equipment is optional, but can be useful when trying to take a dog's vital signs.
- Styptic powder (available at pet stores). This is used to stop bleeding from broken nails.
- Syringe. The size will depend on how big your dog is. Some medications are given in quantities of up to nine teaspoons.
- Towel
- Tweezers
- Wire cutters, small. These can be used to cut the barb off fish hooks embedded in a dog's skin.
- Wooden dowel. These are used as splints and can be cut to the right length for your dog's leg.
- K9 Carrier used to transport your dog. You can find them available at www.K9firstaidandcpr.com

CHAPTER 2
WHAT'S NORMAL?

In order to recognize an emergency when one occurs, it is important to know what's normal for your dog. If you are unsure about a situation, it's always best to call your veterinarian for advice. Many conditions have a better prognosis for recovery if caught early.

It is important to realize that dogs, like children, can compensate very well for many injuries, which means that by the time your dog begins to show signs of a problem, he may already be in an advanced stage of injury or illness.

I am an instructor for Pediatric Advanced Life Support (PALS) and have the pleasure of training new paramedics in this area. The "pediatric assessment triangle" is one of the core components of the PALS instruction course. Assessment of a sick child is based on a quick examination of their appearance, breathing, and circulation. Appearance involves such things as the child's skin tone, how interactive the child is, if they are consolable, their gaze, and the quality of their speech or other vocalizations. These tools allow us to quickly assess if a child is experiencing a life-threatening event, even if he or she is unable to communicate, regarding their symptoms. This same approach can also be useful when it comes to treating dogs.

In order to determine a dog's status, it's important to understand each of the areas assessed when using the pediatric assessment triangle and how they apply to dogs.

Appearance
Since dogs are unable to talk, familiarity with a dog's normal condition—including how the dog walks, eats, urinates, sleeps, breathes, and its overall mood or personality—is crucial when assessing a possible emergency situation. Record your pet's vital signs when healthy and keep this information in your first-aid kit for reference in the case of an emergency. If you notice a change in your dog's personality or eating habits, there is probably a good reason for the change. If your dog was playing and is suddenly depressed or just not acting right, there may be poison involved. This is especially true if the dog is vomiting.

Many treatments and assessments can be done with the dog sitting upright. or laying down. If the dog needs to be on his side, I encourage you to always lay him down on his right side. This will do two things. First, it will bring the dog's heart closer to your hands in case you find it necessary to perform CPR. Second, it will help you to remember to place

WHAT'S NORMAL?

your dog in the same position every time you treat him. If you find yourself wondering "which way is right?" remember that you've said the word *right*, and therefore that's the side you should lay your dog on.

Breathing

Your dog's breathing should always be effortless. Watch her chest rise and fall as she inhales and exhales. Listen for any shallow or gasping sounds and feel the breath coming from your dog's mouth. Write down how many times per minute your dog breathes. While at rest, normal breathing rates are twelve to twenty breaths per minute. A dog who is hot, or has been panting may have up to 200 pants (breathing with his mouth open and tongue out) per minute. That my be normal if the dog was just running. Any number under or over the normal that range could mean there is a problem if the dog is at rest.

Circulation

Circulation is the movement of blood through the body. Without circulation, the brain does not receive the necessary oxygen and sugar it needs to survive. Circulation is evaluated in two ways: checking the mucus membranes and the heart rate.

The heart rate is how many times per minute the heart beats. You can take this measurement by feel, or you can listen with a stethoscope.

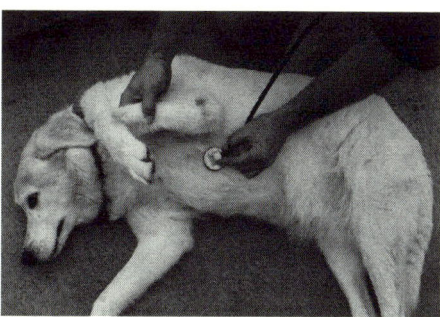

Place the bell of the stethoscope under the dog's armpit area.

K9 MEDIC

To use a stethoscope, place the bell under the dog's front legs in the armpit area. Once you hear the heartbeat, count how many times it beats per minute. To feel for a dog's heart rate, place your hand directly in the armpit area. Some dogs have a bounding (strong) heartbeat than can easily be counted in this way.

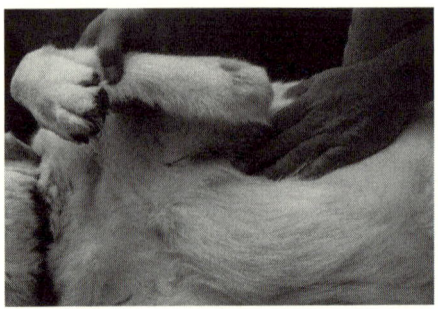

If a dog has a strong, bounding heartbeat, you will be able to feel it by placing your hand in the dog's armpit.

There are a few other locations where you can find a dog's heart rate. You can feel just below the ankle (the part of the body called the hock). To do this, have your dog sit or lie down. Locate the area just below the ankle on the top side of either hind paw. Lightly place your middle and index fingers at this point.

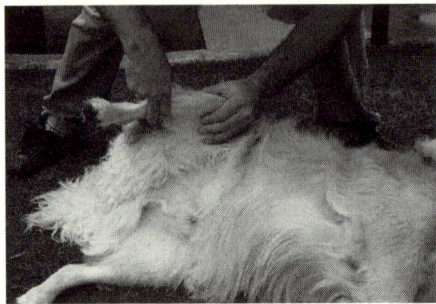

The pulse is usually located on the inner part of the leg.

WHAT'S NORMAL?

A more common place to check a dog's pulse is on the inner thigh. First lay your dog down and lift the upper hind leg away from the lower hind leg. Place two fingers as high up as possible on the inside of either leg, just where the leg meets the body wall. Feel for a recess in the middle of the leg, approximately halfway between the front and back of the leg; this recess is where you will find the pulse.

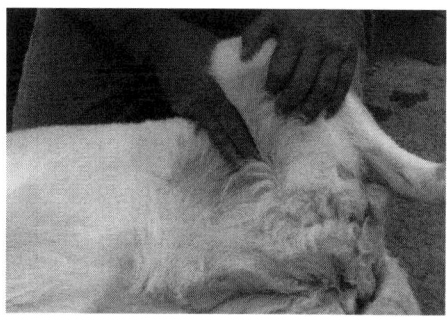

You can also feel the pulse with your fingers.

Using this method can take some time, as you may have to use varied finger pressure and move your hand to locate the blood vessels and accurately feel the pulse. Once you find the pulse, count the number of beats in a minute. A dog's normal heart rate should be between 60 and 140 beats per minute. This tends to be a little higher for puppies. Again, any heart rate that is lower or higher than this range indicates a possible problem. It is important to record your dog's normal heart rate and keep the information in a place where you can easily access it in case of an emergency.

Another way to assess your dog's condition is to check his mucus membranes. This will give you an immediate indication of how well your dog's body systems are working.

K9 MEDIC

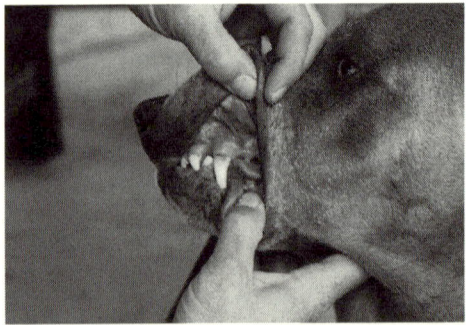

Lift up the lips and be ready to push gently above the canine tooth.

When you lift your dog's lips, you should see pink, healthy gums. Press on the gums with the tip of your finger. This will temporarily press the blood out of the dog's capillaries. When you release your finger, you will see a white spot where you pressed down.

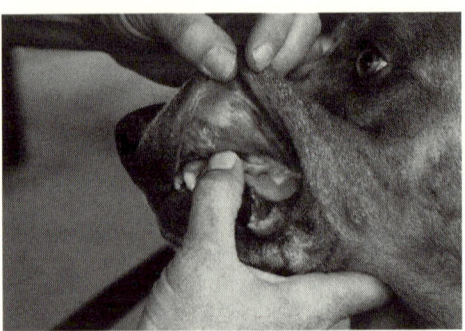

Press for a few seconds, just enough to push
the blood out of the capillaries.

WHAT'S NORMAL?

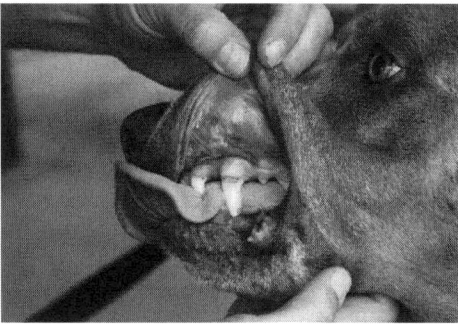

The white color should return to pink within two seconds.

The spot should return to its normal color within two seconds. This is called capillary refill time. If the return of the pink color takes longer than two seconds, it can be an indication of a problem and the dog should be evaluated by a veterinarian ASAP. If your dog's gums are pale, white, cherry red, brown, or blue in color, there may be a problem. This is usually an indicator of shock. Your dog needs immediate attention by a veterinarian.

If your dog's normal gum color is black rather than pink, you should perform this test using the dog's lower eyelid instead. Make sure the membrane of the eyelid is moist. A dry membrane could indicate a dog may be in shock, or dehydrated.

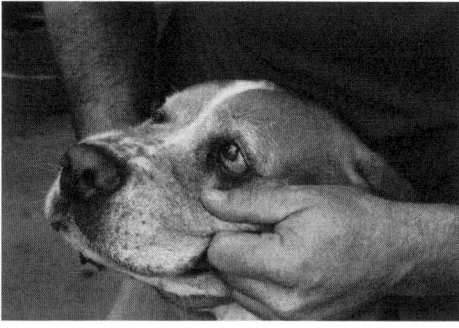

Pull the skin below the eye down. The tissue should be healthy and pink.

K9 MEDIC

Temperature

Another good indicator of your dog's condition is her normal body temperature. Normal body temperature for a dog is between 100°F and 102.5°F. A temperature lower or higher than this range is an emergency; call your veterinarian at once.

Taking your dog's temperature is quite easy. The best type of thermometer to use is a pediatric digital thermometer. These are fairly inexpensive and can be purchased at any drug store.

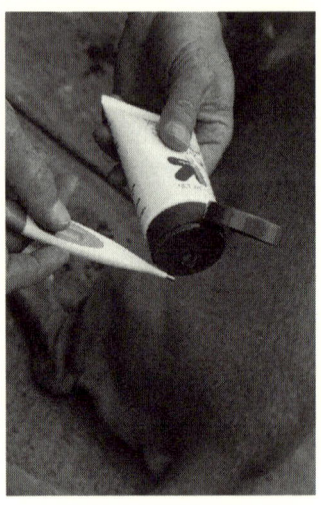

Be sure to lubricate the tip of the thermometer
with a water-based lubricant.

Lubricate the thermometer with a water-based lubricant or petroleum jelly. Insert the tip of the thermometer into the rectum, just beneath the tail. Keep the thermometer inserted until it beeps. Remove and read the number. Clean carefully for next use. Another useful tip is to be sure to mark "Dog" on it.

WHAT'S NORMAL?

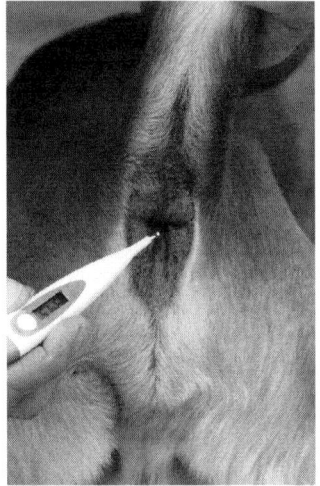

Be careful not to insert the thermometer too deeply into the dog's rectum.

CHAPTER 3
APPROACHING AN INJURED DOG

Before approaching an injured dog, you must first evaluate the scene. Look around for hazards that could potentially harm you. Paramedics call this "scene safety." You have to ask yourself what types of hazards could be present and harmful to an injured dog and/or to you as a rescuer.

If you are on a roadway, you may have to make sure traffic is stopped. Or, if possible, you may need to safely stop traffic yourself.

APPROACHING AN INJURED DOG

Keep in mind that a dog's normal response to injury is to get up and run away. This is an attempt to get away from whatever danger caused the injury. Do not assume that a dog is not injured just because he is able to leave the scene. You must always assume that the dog is severely injured in order to proceed safely.

When approaching an injured dog, there are some basic principles to which any caregiver must adhere. Safely approaching and restraining any dog that is conscious and appears to be ill or injured is an essential part of ensuring your safety. Remember to talk to the injured dog using a soft voice. This will help the dog stay calm. Many dogs are comforted by hearing a quiet, soothing voice. What you say is not important; rather, the tone of voice is all that really matters.

Always approach a sick or injured dog slowly and cautiously from the side. Never approach form head on. Even your own animal might strike out if frightened or in pain. It would be nice if dogs were able to tell us where it hurts, but let's face it: that's not the case. We must treat them as if they have an injury even before we are certain about what's wrong. Imagine having broken bones in your arm and someone coming up and grabbing you, wanting to help but instead causing even more pain. When treating an injured dog, caregivers must proceed with caution in order to avoid these kinds of mistakes.

The first thing to do is to observe the posture and expression of the dog, especially the face, ears, tail, fur, and body. As you approach, listen to the sounds he is making. Is he grunting? Or whimpering in pain? Is there any bleeding that you can see? Is your dog favoring one leg over the other?

As you approach, allow the dog to smell the back of your hand. Never sit down. If the dog suddenly turns aggressive, you will have no where to get away. This is more true if it's a dog who you do not know. Even though you may have been caring for this dog since he was a puppy, you must reestablish your connection and let the dog know that you are friendly and not an enemy. Avoid quick or jerky movements or loud sounds. Allow the dog to see what you are doing and watch his reactions carefully. Always speak in a soft, soothing tone to an injured or sick animal, just as you would to a child. Avoid direct eye contact, as some dogs may perceive this as a threat.

Again, your safety is the top priority. Once you have made the decision to help, you must be extremely careful to avoid being bitten. Watch for behaviors that signal that a dog may bite:

- Ears held forward
- Tail wagging slightly
- Growling
- Fur standing up on shoulders, back, and hind end
- Snarling with upper lips lifted and teeth exposed
- Crouching with tail between hind legs
- Ears held straight back or flat against the head
- Snarling with fur on the back raised
- Assuming a submissive posture (lying on her side with her belly exposed, making licking gestures, or urinating)

What should you do if an animal is exhibiting any of these behaviors? Sadly, the answer is that you must not attempt treatment on any dog showing these behaviors. While it may be distressing to withhold treatment from the animal, the risk is simply too great at that point. If you cannot safely handle an animal, call your local animal control agency. They are better prepared to deal with such a situation.

CHAPTER 4
RESTRAINING AND MUZZLING AN INJURED DOG

The term restrain means: a: to prevent from doing, exhibiting, or expressing something. b: to limit, restrict, or keep under control. Once a dog has allowed you to approach, you should next restrain the animal. Keep in mind that you will have to use different techniques depending on the size of the dog. For example, you can restrain a Maltese terrier with nothing more than a towel. A Great Dane, however, might very well eat a towel. With large breeds, a leash is necessary to safely restrain the animal.

When restraining a dog using a towel, avoid putting your hands near the dog's mouth. Instead, drop a large towel or blanket onto the dog from above and behind. Then grab the scruff of the neck so the dog cannot turn around and bite your hand through the towel. Move the dog to a carrier.

To safely use a leash to restrain a dog, first make a large loop in a leash by passing the end you normally connect to the collar through the hole in the handle.

Pass the clip through the loop at the end of the leash.

Then drop this large loop over the dog's neck and tighten. Be careful: since you are actually creating something like a makeshift noose, you can accidentally choke the dog if you pull too tightly. You never want to cause the dog to have trouble breathing. If the dog is calm and will allow you to clip the leash on the collar normally, you can use that method as well.

RESTRAINING AND MUZZLING AN INJURED DOG

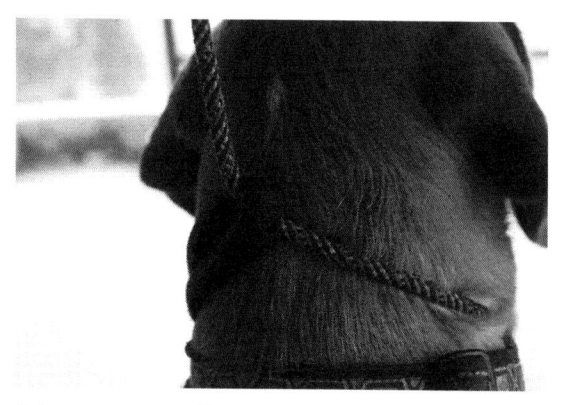

Be careful, as constant pulling can actually choke and injure the dog.

After the dog is restrained, he must be muzzled. Muzzling is done strictly for your safety. Even the most well-behaved dog may bite if frightened or hurt. Do not assume that wearing thick gloves will protect you from bites. Most dogs can bite through almost any gloves. Wearing gloves can also cause you to lose manual dexterity.

One important guideline to keep in mind when muzzling is that more is *not* better. The *least* amount of restraint that will be effective should be applied. Excessive restraint becomes a test of wills between you and the dog, and you will find dogs to be stubborn and unrelenting. The more you attempt to restrain them, the harder they resist and the less pleasant and more dangerous the experience becomes for both the human and the animal. Using excessive force can even injure a dog further. Using a muzzle reduces the need for additional restraint. Once the muzzle is in place, the dog may stop struggling. It is also equally important to have the right muzzle. Working dogs, and dogs that have been involved in recent exertion should have a muzzle that will allow the dog to breath with their mouth open as illustrated below. You can do great harm in closing a dogs mouth who needs to pant/breathe.

It is important to practice muzzling your dog from time to time even when he is not injured. Dog owners should do this at least once a week until their dog is completely comfortable with being muzzled. Do not wait until you have a stressful event to try to introduce your dog to the muzzle.

Always remember that no muzzle is foolproof. You may have one of those dogs that can escape even the best muzzle. Do not let your guard down.

The point at which you muzzle a dog will depend on the situation at hand. You will want to muzzle the dog if you have the slightest concern that she might bite you, or if the dog is in such pain that she will not let you do an initial evaluation. Always muzzle an injured dog before doing an evaluation. If you can evaluate the dog without the muzzle, be sure to muzzle her before treating or moving the animal.

Muzzling a dog reduces the chances of caregivers being bitten. However, it also puts our four-legged friend at risk. When you apply a muzzle, you must be prepared to remove it, sometimes very quickly. There are times when a muzzle does more harm than good. If any of the conditions discussed below exist, you must remove the muzzle immediately.

Some muzzles have a quick release at the top of the muzzle.

RESTRAINING AND MUZZLING AN INJURED DOG

If the dog is having difficulty breathing, a muzzle will only make the situation worse. You will need to keep the dog's mouth clear and allow him to obtain all the air he can.

If the dog is coughing, it is a sign that she may soon vomit. Vomiting is one of the worst things that can happen when a dog is muzzled. This creates the risk of the dog inhaling the vomit, pulling it into her lungs. This could lead to immediate suffocation or cause the dog to develop pneumonia.

Homemade muzzles can be made from materials found in your first-aid kit and can be used on most breed types. For example, if a muzzle is not available, a length of rolled gauze will suffice. Dogs have very powerful jaw muscles that can close with force up to 300 psi. Opening, however, is a different story. A simple gauze muzzle can prevent even large-breed dogs from opening their jaws.

I like to use Kerlix, as the gauze should *not* be stretchy. The length must be adequate to wrap around the muzzle at least twice and then tie behind the ears. Start with three feet of Kerlix.

Be sure you have a piece long enough to create the muzzle.

Form a large loop and a loose knot in the middle of the gauze. The loop should be about three times the diameter of the dog's muzzle.

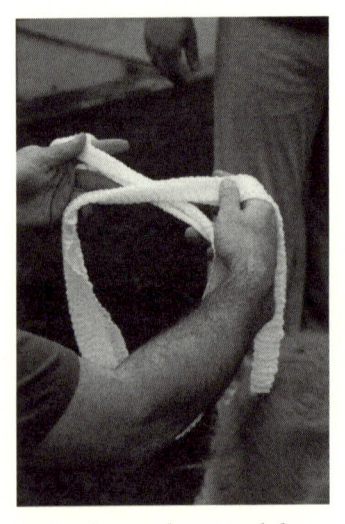

Make a loop and tie a single knot.

Place the knot around the muzzle, pulling it tight on the top of the nose. Be sure not to over-tighten.

Do not over-tighten the top knot.

RESTRAINING AND MUZZLING AN INJURED DOG

Next, cross the ends of the gauze under the dog's jaw. Then bring the long ends of the gauze behind the ears and tie them in either a square knot or an easy-release bow. I prefer to tie a square knot and have scissors handy in case I need to remove the muzzle quickly.

Be sure to cross the ends before you pull them back to tie.

Please note that this style of muzzle can easily slip off breeds with a short face. To reduce slippage, after tying the square knot behind the ears, bring the long ends of the gauze forward and loop the ends under the loop of gauze around the muzzle. Pull the ends back over the forehead and under the gauze behind the ears. Then tie another square knot.

Tie the knot to complete the muzzle.
You may now start treating the animal.

If you prefer a store-bought muzzle rather than a homemade one, the most important factor is purchasing the correct size for your dog. Muzzles are quite affordable and usually have a sizing chart located on the back of the package.

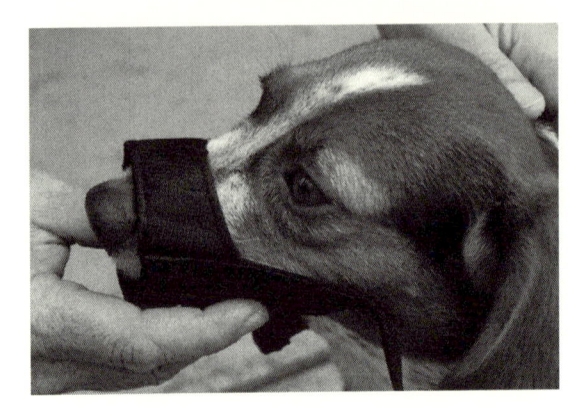

Be sure to purchase a correctly sized muzzle, as this
will reduce the chances of the dog being able to escape it.

RESTRAINING AND MUZZLING AN INJURED DOG

Measure your dog to determine her correct muzzle size. Start at the dog's eye and measure down to the tip of the nose to get an accurate muzzle length. To measure for the proper circumference, start one inch below the eye and measure all the way around the dog's nose. For proper muzzle fit, you must add length to each circumference measurement. An additional one-fourth of an inch to half of an inch is required for a small dog. Large dogs require an additional half inch to one full inch. If all this seems confusing, simply look at the back of the package. Many muzzle packages list specific breeds and the muzzle size they usually require.

The two main types of dog muzzles are the basket type and the occlusion type. Basket muzzles allow the dog to pant freely and drink water while wearing the muzzle. Basket muzzles are good for long-term use when the dog is outside. Occlusion muzzles keep the dog's mouth almost completely shut. These are only advised for short-term use.

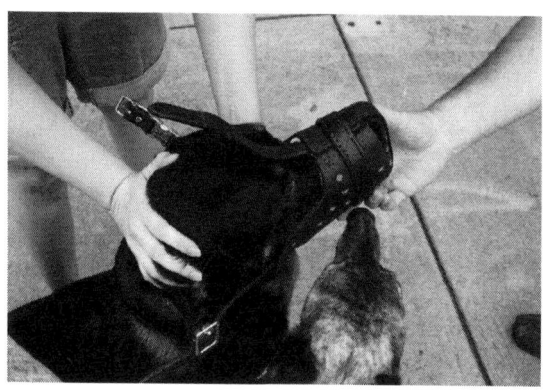

An occlusion muzzle may be necessary when a dog needs to visit a veterinarian.

If you are going to purchase a muzzle, be sure to examine the different materials available and choose the one you prefer for your dog. Dog muzzles come in a variety of materials that vary in price and aesthetic appeal. Basket dog muzzles come in heavy-duty wire (the choice preferred for aggressive, untrained dogs), leather (strong and attractive but expensive), and plastic (affordable and a good choice for less aggressive dogs). There are also soft nylon muzzles available. Each type of muzzle will have its own set of instructions that will show you the proper way to place it on your dog.

For short-nosed dogs, mesh muzzles are available that actually cover the dog's face. These are also sometimes called grooming muzzles. These muzzles are designed to restrict aggressive behavior while allowing short-nosed dogs to breathe normally. They are even safe for use on dogs with breathing problems. One size fits most when it comes to these muzzles.

If you do not have a muzzle for a short-nosed dog, you can easily create a restraint using a towel. Roll up a towel and place it around the dog's neck. The dog will not be able to move his head very much, keeping you out of harm's way.

Once you have the dog muzzled, you can provide first aid.

CAUTION: Some muzzles that keep the dogs mouth closed can inhibit their ability to pant and expel their heat. Dogs rely on panting as their primary means for getting rid of excess body heat. Panting allows evaporation of water and heat across the moist surfaces of the lungs, tongue, and surfaces within the mouth. It is important this process is allowed to happen or would could send the dog into heat stroke which could be fatal.

RESTRAINING AND MUZZLING AN INJURED DOG

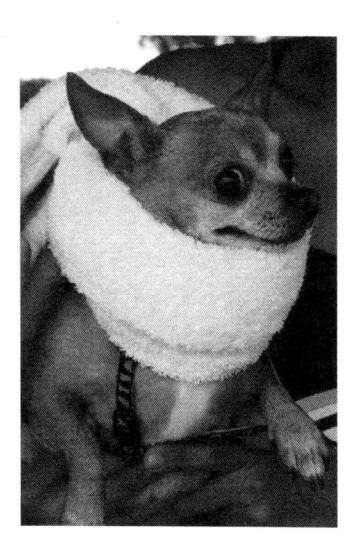

A towel can easily be used to muzzle a small dog.

There are times when you may need to prevent a large dog from turning or attempting to overpower you in order to provide aid. In such situations, having two people available to provide care is ideal, as one of you can hold the dog while the other provides first aid. You can secure your dog by placing your forearm under the dog's neck and wrapping your arm around his head. Firmly lock your forearm under the dog's head. Place your other arm over or under his belly. Just think of this as a big hug.

When using this technique be particularly careful with small dogs with pushed-in noses, such as pugs; some breeds have weak eye muscles and holding the neck too tightly can cause the eyes to pop out of their sockets in some breeds.

CHAPTER 5
ARTIFICIAL RESPIRATION, CHEST COMPRESSIONS AND CPR

If a dog's breathing ceases, or the heart stops, the brain will not receive the oxygen and sugar the body needs to live. This is why it is crucial to deal with any situation involving impaired breathing immediately. When providing artificial respiration, chest compressions, or CPR, there is only a small window of time in which you can help your pet.

ARTIFICIAL RESPIRATION, CHEST COMPRESSIONS AND CPR

Let's say you wake up to find your dog lifeless and not breathing. Even if you start CPR immediately, the chances are extremely low that you will be able to reverse the dying process. In most cases, you have no way of knowing when your dog stopped breathing. If you last saw your dog normal and alert last night, and it's now 9:00 a.m. the next morning, chances are the death process happened several hours ago and any chance of survival may be considered to be futile.

In humans, for every minute that goes by in which someone is not breathing and no one is performing CPR, the chance of survival drops 10 percent. Let's do some math. If I was to collapse at noon and nobody performed CPR in the first five minutes, I would have only a 50 percent chance of survival. If eight minutes went by and no one performed CPR, I would have only a 20 percent chance of survival. If eleven minutes passed, CPR could not save my life. What does this mean for dog owners? Our best chance for a good outcome is when we actually witness our pet's breathing stop. This is an example of just how delicate life is.

Of course, since there is no 911 for dogs, your pet's treatment and the decision regarding whether to transport him for further medical care will be up to you. As a responsible pet owner, you need to have a "CPR Plan" in place *before* an emergency occurs. This will take some of the stress and guess work out of an emergency.

When making your CPR Plan, it is critical to limit the number of interruptions you will experience while performing CPR. Remember, any interruption to CPR will mean your dog's brain is not getting oxygen.

One of the first decisions you will have to make as part of your plan is whether or not to take the dog to the vet. Many dog owners are surprised to learn that staying home and doing good CPR may be is often the best option. in the event of an emergency. Any time that you are not doing good compressions the dog and vital organs are dying. There are several reasons for this. If you have a large dog (over 75 pounds), simply getting her into your vehicle can prove quite challenging. Unless you can count on having two or three people present to help load the dog into your vehicle, plan on staying home and performing CPR.

Another reason to avoid transporting your dog is that it could mean interrupting CPR. If you are alone, you might be forced to drive a few blocks, stop to perform CPR for a minute, then drive a few blocks more, repeating this sequence until you reach your destination. Obviously, having two people in the vehicle would be more practical, as one person could drive while the other performs CPR. Regardless of your situation, always obey traffic laws and do not put yourself or others in harm's way by driving recklessly.

Another factor to consider when making your CPR Plan is that CPR can be very exhausting. Many people become too tired to continue while performing CPR, especially if they are doing so alone. If this should happen to you, know that it is OK. Try to find comfort in the fact that you did everything in your power to save your dog.

You may attempt to perform CPR for up to twenty minutes, or until you see some kind of response. This could be as minor as the dog breathing on his own or moving an extremity. If you do not see any improvement in the dog's condition after twenty minutes, it is unlikely that she is going to survive. As heartbreaking as it may be, this is the time to consider stopping CPR. The exception to this twenty-minute rule is if your dog has been involved in a cold-water drowning; in these situations, paramedics sometimes see people survive even after being submerged for more than an hour.

If the dog does respond, do not expect her to get up and immediately return to her normal behavior. Any dog that survives CPR is still a very sick canine and will need medical attention.

ARTIFICIAL RESPIRATION, CHEST COMPRESSIONS AND CPR

Artificial Respiration

Your dog's breathing should always be effortless. Like humans, when dogs breathe, their diaphragm needs to move downward; this draws air into the lungs. When an animal stops breathing, the diaphragm relaxes in the "up" position, leaving the lungs empty. Why is this important? Whether breathing for a dog or a human being, performing CPR means filling the lungs with air again.

In order to know when your dog is having a breathing emergency, you must first know what normal breathing looks like. First, watch the dog inhale and exhale. Count the number of times that the chest rises and falls in a minute. If the chest does not rise and fall or if the abdomen expands, it is an emergency. Remember that exhaling should be effortless. Loud, shallow, or gasping sounds when breathing indicate an emergency. These sounds could be symptoms of an airway blockage.

Always place the dog on his right side when providing treatment. This will bring the heart closer to your hands.

If the dog is not breathing, lay him down on his *right* side. Keep the head in a neutral position. Try to imagine an invisible line from the dog's mouth to his lungs. You want this line to be as straight as possible (that is what a "neutral position" means).

When a dog is unconscious, her tongue becomes flaccid (limp). Pull the tongue forward (it's OK if it sticks out of the mouth and hangs down).

The tongue will pull out quite far.

Next, wrap both hands and your fingers around the snout, closing the mouth gently. If you do not do this, air will escape when you breathe into the dog.

Next, place your mouth over the dog's nostrils. By doing so, you are creating a seal, which is crucial to properly performing CPR. With small dogs, you may have to place your mouth over the entire nose.

You must seal your lips around the dog's nostrils.

ARTIFICIAL RESPIRATION, CHEST COMPRESSIONS AND CPR

Now breathe softly into the dog's nose, watching as the chest rises. You should blow in as much air as it takes to slowly raise the chest. Keep in mind that with a small dog, the amount of air needed will be much smaller. Once you remove your mouth, the chest should fall. Repeat this twice.

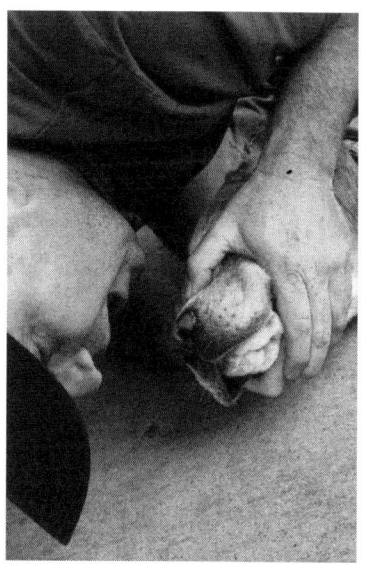

You must wrap your hands around the mouth
to prevent air from leaking out.

If for some reason you blow and do not see the chest rise, the first and most simple thing to do is to check your mouth placement to make sure that you are covering the dog's nostrils and creating a good seal. Another possibility is that something is lodged in the dog's throat. (See choking, chapter 8.) If for whatever reason you are unable to get air into the dog, you can still give the animal a fighting chance by doing chest compressions only.

There may be times when your dog has a heartbeat but is not breathing. This is when you need to preform rescue breathing.

Simply breathe into the snout every six to eight seconds until your dog starts to breathe on his own or you are able to seek medical attention.

Chest Compressions
Did you know that you have a reserve of oxygen in your system? If you were to collapse and stop breathing, you would just need someone to move this oxygen around for you. This means performing chest compressions. Chest compressions squeeze the heart, causing blood to flow through the body.

Have you taken a CPR class during the past ten years? If so, you know that the proper procedures can change quite frequently as medical science evolves. Today's motto is "Push Hard and Push Fast." What's fast? Today's human CPR guidelines instruct care providers to perform between 100 and 120 compressions per minute.

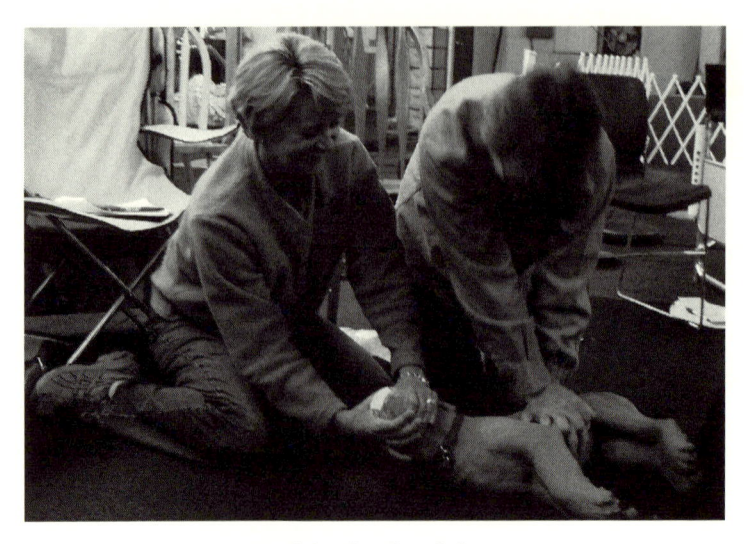

Push hard and push fast.

ARTIFICIAL RESPIRATION, CHEST COMPRESSIONS AND CPR

Not only must compressions be fast, they must also be hard—meaning a minimum of two inches in depth. I have seen healthcare providers push close to half the depth of a person's chest. Of course, compressions need to be deeper in bigger people, and this is also true for dogs. Compression depth is always relative to size.

To determine how deep compressions need to be for a dog, look at how many inches there are between the widest parts of the animal's shoulders. The correct compression depth is 1/3 to 1/2 of that measurement.

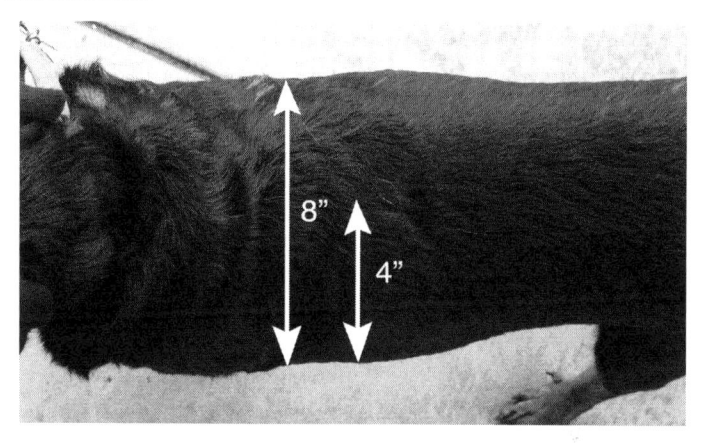

With a large dog, you will need to compress four inches.

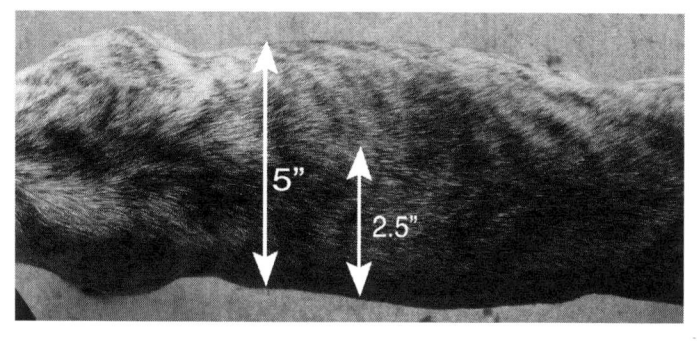

With smaller-chested dogs, you do not need to press as deeply.

When it comes to doing CPR on dogs, we increase the compression rate to 120 times per minute, or twice per second.

How can you be sure that your dog requires chest compressions? Perform compressions only if the dog is unconscious and not breathing. The best way to determine if a dog is unconscious is to attempt to touch his eyelids. If the animal is unconscious, you will not see any flickering or the eyes attempting to shut when poking gently at the eyelid. This is a life-threatening emergency.

Always check for a heartbeat or pulse before starting chest compressions. If the animal is conscious and responds to you, the heart is beating and you should not perform chest compressions. Do not assume that there is no heartbeat or pulse simply because an animal is not breathing.

The following steps should be followed to perform chest compressions on any dog over twenty pounds. Smaller dogs are covered later in the chapter.

1. Lay the dog on its *right* side, and kneel at the dog's side.
2. Rotate the front leg of the dog onto its chest. Your hands should be placed where the dog's elbow meets its body.

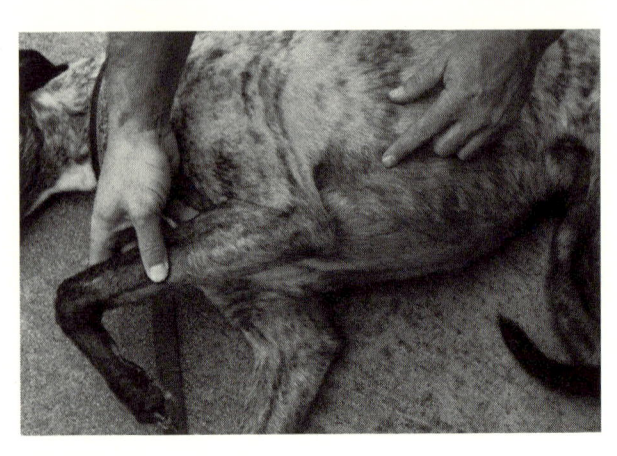

The heart is directly under this location.

ARTIFICIAL RESPIRATION, CHEST COMPRESSIONS AND CPR

3. Place the heel of your hand on that spot. Place your other hand on top of the one that is in position. Be sure to keep your fingers up off the chest wall. You may find it easier to do this if you interlock your fingers.
4. Bring your shoulders directly over the dog. You will want to stay at a 90-degree angle.

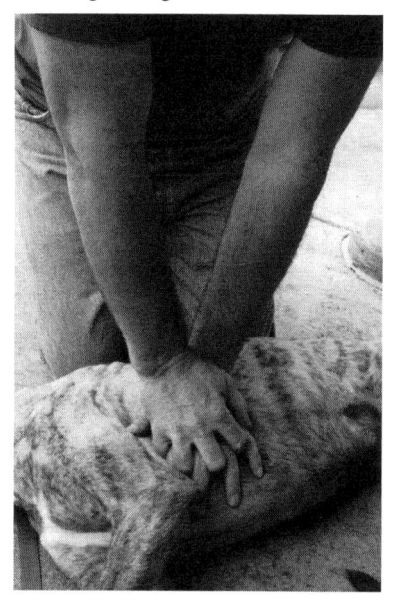

After the first few compressions,
you will feel the rib cartilage crack. Keep going!

5. Keeping your arms straight, press down. Push hard and fast. It's important for the dog's heart to fill back up prior to pushing down again. To ensure you are doing it correctly, each compression should start with your hands resting on the dog's fur. Push down the proper depth, and then return to the start position.
6. Avoid interruptions in chest compressions (to prevent stoppage of blood flow).

K9 MEDIC

7. Push hard and fast 120 times per minute. Remember to push down 1/3 to 1/2 as deep as the dog's body.

For dogs less than ten pounds, follow the steps below (which are similar to performing chest compressions on a human child):

1. Holding the dog in your arms, turn her upside down.
2. Take two fingers and place them on the breastbone between the two front legs.

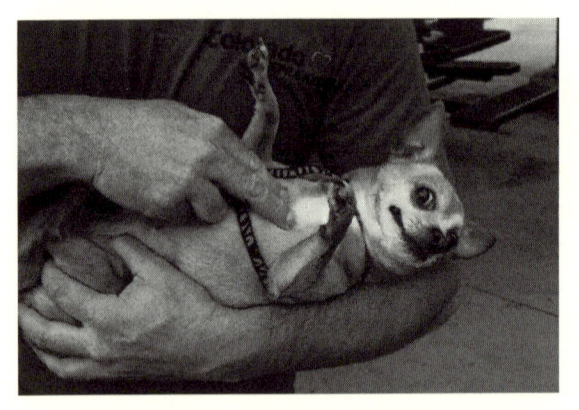

Press on the breastbone, 1/3 to 1/2 the depth of the dog's chest.

3. Push down, 1/3 to 1/2 the depth of the dog's chest, repeating the action quickly (120 times per minute).
4. Remember, relaxation and compression should be of equal duration. Avoid interruptions in chest compressions to prevent stoppage of blood flow.

ARTIFICIAL RESPIRATION, CHEST COMPRESSIONS AND CPR

CPR

Cardiopulmonary resuscitation (CPR) is a combination of artificial respiration and chest compressions. CPR is used to treat an animal that is not breathing and has no heartbeat or pulse. In general, there are three situations in which it may be necessary to perform CPR on a dog: smoke inhalation, electrocution, or drowning.

As with chest compressions, always check for a heartbeat or pulse before starting CPR. If the animal is conscious and responds to you, the heart is beating and you should not perform CPR. Do not assume that there is no heartbeat or pulse simply because an animal is not breathing.

Unfortunately, there is a lot of contradictory information out there regarding the ratio of how many compressions to breaths to provide during CPR. As a firm believer in keeping things simple, I teach my students one easy-to-remember ratio that can be used on both dogs and humans: thirty compressions to two breaths. You can use this same ratio regardless of the size of the dog, how many people are with you, or any other factors. I can tell you from working as a paramedic that we are saving more people today than ever before, and one big reason for this is uninterrupted compressions. The more time you can spend doing compressions, the more blood will flow through the body. Remember, compressions should be performed at a rate of 120 times per minute.

The following steps should be followed to perform CPR on any dog ten pounds or smaller. Larger dogs are covered later in the chapter.

1. Make sure the scene is safe.
2. Check to see if the dog is breathing and whether or not it has a heartbeat or pulse. If the dog is not breathing and has no heartbeat, begin CPR.
3. Place the dog on a hard surface or hold him in your arms, and turn him upside-down.
4. Give two breaths (as explained earlier in the chapter).
5. Wrap your hands around the dog's body so your thumb is on the breastbone, or the center of the chest.
6. Push down 1/3 to 1/2 the depth of the chest very quickly. Remember, you will need to maintain a pace of 120 compressions per minute.
7. Do not take your thumbs or fingers off the dog's body.
8. Repeat pushing and count to thirty. (If you are nervous and lose count, don't worry. You are doing the best you can given the difficulty of the situation.)
9. After thirty compressions, again give two breaths.
10. Repeat this sequence.

The following steps explain how to perform CPR on any dog larger than ten pounds:

1. Make sure the scene is safe.
2. Check to see whether the dog is breathing and has a heartbeat or pulse. If the dog is not breathing and has no heartbeat, begin CPR.

ARTIFICIAL RESPIRATION, CHEST COMPRESSIONS AND CPR

3. Lay the dog on her right side and put her head in a neutral position.
4. Give two breaths (as explained earlier in the chapter).
5. Rotate the dog's front leg to her chest. Place your hands where the dog's elbow meets its body. Place the lower part of your palm on the dog's chest and bring your shoulders directly over the dog. You will want to stay at a 90-degree angle.
6. Push down 1/3 to 1/2 the depth of the chest very quickly. Remember, you will need to maintain a pace of at least 100 compressions per minute.
7. Do not take your hands off the dog's chest, but be sure to let the chest come back to its natural position between compressions.
8. Repeat pushing and count to thirty.
9. After thirty compressions, give two breaths.
10. Repeat the sequence.

When CPR Fails

When a dog is in a situation in which CPR is required, he is very sick. These situations often end in death. After all, CPR cannot turn back the aging process, trauma, cancer, or other serious illnesses. But even when CPR is unsuccessful, many dog owners find peace in knowing that they did everything they could to help save their dog. If you perform CPR on your dog and he passes away despite your efforts, do not carry around guilt or wonder if there was anything more that you could have done. Measure your success on your effort, not the outcome. Even with todays advanced medicine; Statistics show for a out of hospital cardiac arrest witnessed by a healthcare provider your chances of survival are around 28%.

Students sometimes ask me if a dog can be too old to receive CPR. In my opinion, this is a personal choice. I personally would not perform CPR on a dog who was nearing the end of her natural life or who had some form of incurable disease or illness. I would find peace in knowing when it's time to say good-bye.

CHAPTER 6
CHOKING

Choking is actually the number one cause of trauma and death in dogs. Acting quickly can be the difference between life and death in a choking situation. Dogs often swallow objects accidentally, and these "foreign objects" can easily become lodged in the animal's throat. Such objects can block the airway either partially or completely.

I often tell my students that when a dog is choking, you are on the "choking highway," and there are only two exits. The first exit is removing the object so your dog can breathe again. The second exit is not as pleasant. If your dog is unable to breathe, he will attempt to get the object out until he uses up the limited amount of oxygen left in his system. At that point, you will need to perform CPR. You can only hope that performing compressions will dislodge the object. Before performing CPR, be sure to look in your dog's mouth for the object. If you can pull it out, do so.

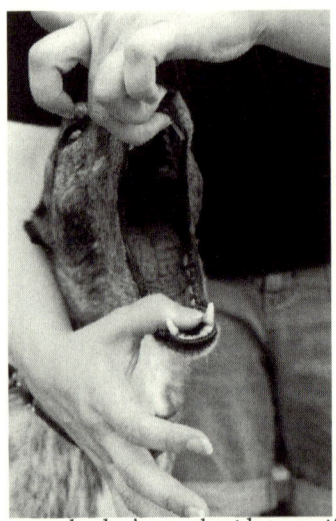

You may need to open the dog's mouth wide to see if you can remove the object. However, be cautious when performing this action, as this increases your chances of being bitten.

If your dog is still able to cough, it may mean that she is getting a limited amount of air. What would it look like if she had a complete obstruction?
1. The dog might paw at the mouth.
2. The dog's gums will turn blue or white.
3. The dog might make gasping noises as she attempts to breathe.
4. The dog might cough up white mucus.
5. There might be excessive drooling.

CHOKING

6. The dog might become frantic.
7. The dog's eyes might bulge out.
8. The dog might stop breathing.
9. The dog might collapse.

When a dog is choking, there is little time to waste. The good news is that choking victims can often be treated successfully on the scene. As a paramedic, I respond to many choking calls per year. Rarely do I find the patient still needs my assistance. This is usually because someone on the scene had performed the Heimlich maneuver.

The Heimlich maneuver is an emergency procedure for removing a foreign object lodged in the airway that is preventing a person (or dog) from breathing. Dr. Henry Heimlich first described an emergency technique for expelling foreign material blocking the trachea in 1974. This technique, now called the Heimlich maneuver, is simple enough that it can be performed with very little training. The Heimlich maneuver is a standard part of all first-aid courses.

The theory behind the Heimlich maneuver is that by compressing the abdomen below the level of the diaphragm, air is forced out of the lungs under pressure, dislodging any obstruction in the trachea and bringing the foreign material back up into the mouth. In human infants and dogs, this can also be accomplished by delivering a blow to the back. The Heimlich maneuver can be used when solid materials such as bones, food, coins, socks, balls, vomit, or small toys are blocking the airway.

Caring for a dog that is conscious and choking can be a challenge. The dog may be frantic and you may not be able to keep them still to look for or attempt to remove the object. Do your best. ·

As with CPR, the Heimlich maneuver is performed differently depending on the size of the dog. The technique should be performed as follows for small dogs (twenty pounds or less):

1. As always, check the scene for safety before providing treatment.
2. Open the dog's mouth, look inside, and pull the tongue forward. If you can see the obstruction, pull it out. Be careful never to place your fingers into the throat blindly, as this can push the object deeper down the dog's throat.
3. If you are unable to remove the object manually, perform back blows. Keeping the dog's head down, deliver a sharp blow with the palm of your hand between the dog's shoulder blades. Repeat this five times.

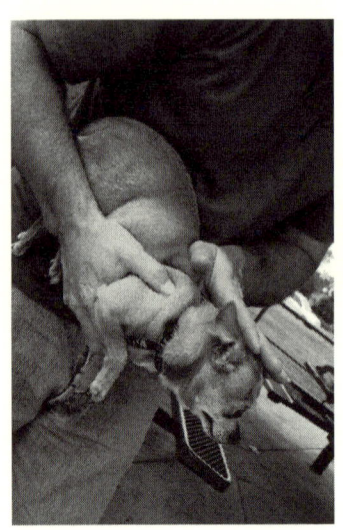

Deliver back blows between the dog's shoulder blades.

4. If the object has still not been dislodged, perform abdominal thrusts. Turn the dog over so the belly is exposed and place two fingers or thumbs on the breastbone. Push hard five times.

CHOKING

Abdominal thrusts are delivered in the same manner as chest thrusts.

5. Repeat this sequence until the object is dislodged or the dog loses consciousness.
6. If the dog loses consciousness, immediately open the mouth and look to see if you can grab the object.
7. Once it is removed or you can not grab it begin CPR.

Adjust the technique as follows for large dogs (over twenty pounds) *if* you can lift up the dog's front legs and torso:

1. Lift the dog by her front legs with her spine against your chest and wrap your arms around the animal under her ribs.

Place your thumb just below the rib cage.

2. Make a fist with one hand and place your other hand over your fist.
3. Deliver five rapid abdominal thrusts, lifting your fist in an inward and upward motion (just as you would with a person).

Pull in and up in a rapid thrusting motion. Repeat until the object comes out or the dog loses consciousness.

4. Repeat the sequence until you remove the object or the dog loses consciousness.
5. If the dog loses consciousness, immediately open the mouth and look to see if you can grab the object.
6. Once it is removed or you can not grab it begin CPR.

You can also deliver abdominal thrusts while standing behind the dog by bending over and wrapping your arms around the animal under the ribs. The dog will be between your legs. I find this stance somewhat awkward, but this can vary from person to person.

CHOKING

Adjust the technique as follows for large dogs (over twenty pounds) if you *cannot* lift up the front legs and torso:

1. Stand behind the dog.
2. If you can, lift up the back legs and deliver five sharp back blows between the shoulder blades.

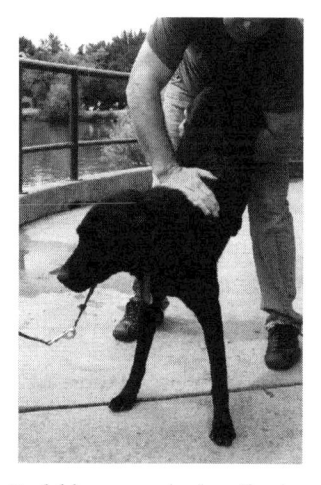

Back blows can also be effective.

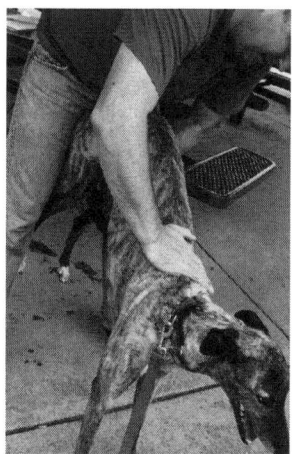

Be sure to keep the dog's head down, as this allows gravity to assist in removing the object.

3. Repeat these steps until the object comes out or the dog loses consciousness. Usually the dog will become limp at this point and appear lifeless. Check the animal's mouth. If you see the object, remove it if possible. If you can not see the object you may choose to place your hand down the dogs throat in attempt to pull it out. Use this step with caution and keep in mind there may be a chance you may be bitten. If the dog loses consciousness, begin CPR.

Do not wait until your dog is choking to find out if you will be able to lift her up while holding her under the ribs. Take the time in a normal situation to familiarize yourself with the position you would need to be in to perform the Heimlich maneuver on your dog. Likewise, take the time to learn where you will need to place your hands in the event of choking *before* you face an emergency. However, do not practice actually performing the Heimlich maneuver on your pet, as this may injure the dog.

If you ever perform the Heimlich maneuver on a dog and are able to remove the foreign object, be sure to take the dog to the vet immediately afterward.

CHAPTER 7
SHOCK

The most important thing you need to understand about the term *shock* is that it means that your dog's internal organs are dying.

A body's cells need two things to function: oxygen and glucose. These substances allow the cells to generate energy and do their specific jobs. Medically, shock is defined as a condition in which the body's tissues are not receiving enough oxygen and glucose to allow the cells to function. This ultimately leads to cellular death, progressing to organ failure, and, finally, death.

Oxygen in the air enters the body through the lungs, where oxygen molecules cross into the smallest blood vessels, called capillaries, and are picked up by red blood cells. The pumping of the heart pushes red blood cells through the body, where they deliver oxygen to cells in all the tissues of the body. These same blood cells then pick up carbon dioxide, the waste product of metabolism, taking it back to the lungs, where it is exhaled out of the body. Then the whole cycle starts again.

Glucose is generated in the body via the digestion of the food we eat. Like oxygen, it travels in the blood stream, providing energy for cellular metabolism.

What does all this mean to you? If your dog is in shock, his internal organs are dying because they are not getting enough oxygen and glucose from the blood.

Shock can result from a sudden loss of blood, a traumatic injury, heart failure, a severe allergic reaction (known as anaphylactic shock), certain types of organ diseases, or a severe infection (known as septic shock).

While it is not necessarily important to know why your dog may be in shock, you do need to be familiar with the signs of shock. This will allow you to react quickly and transport your dog to the veterinarian when necessary.

There are three stages of shock. The animal's symptoms may change drastically as she moves through these stages. During early shock, the body attempts to compensate for the decreased flow of fluids and oxygen to the tissues. During middle shock, the body begins to have difficulty compensating for the lack of blood flow and oxygen. During end-stage shock, the body can no longer compensate for the lack of oxygen and blood flow to vital organs. This often leads to death.

One of the most important indicators of shock is an elevated heart rate. This is because the heart is attempting to beat faster to compensate for some problem or change. The problem may be

SHOCK

that there is not enough blood, or the heart may be failing. A dog in shock may have a heart rate that is elevated to twice its normal level. In dogs, any heart rate of more than 160 beats per minute is an indication of shock. In such a case, take your dog to the vet immediately.

Other indicators of shock include:
1. A drop in body temperature
2. Shivering
3. Depression
4. Weakness
5. Cold paws and legs
6. Pale skin and mucus membranes
7. A weak or faint pulse

In my opinion, the best indicator of shock in a dog is the gums. If your dog has naturally pink gums, they will become pale, white, or even blue if the dog is in shock. To check your dog's gums, press on the gums with the tip of your finger. This will temporarily press the blood out of the dog's capillaries. When you release your finger, you should see a white spot where you pressed down. If you do not see this spot return to normal within two seconds, your dog may be in shock.

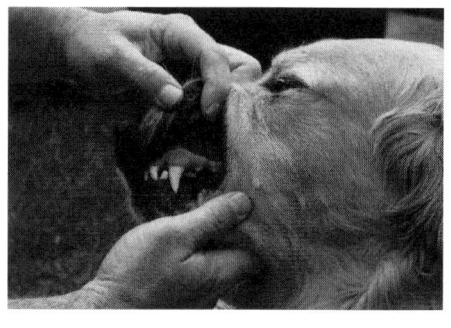

Locate the area just above the canine tooth.

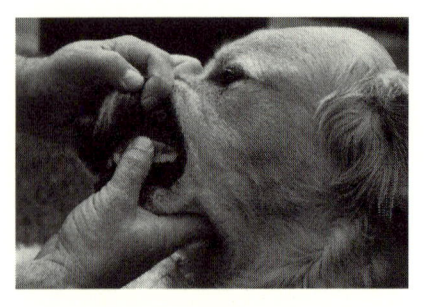

Press and hold for a few seconds.

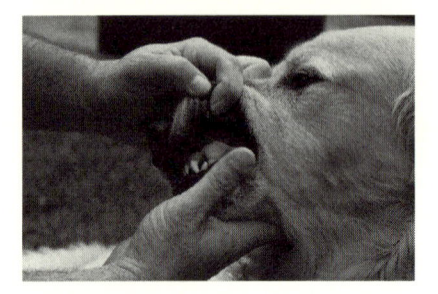

The white spot that appears should return to a normal color within two seconds. If it does not, the dog may be in shock.

Remember, shock is a serious medical condition. It is not your job to try to fix this problem. In the case of shock, you need only to identify it and get your dog help as soon as possible. If you suspect your dog is in shock, proceed as follows:

1. Check to see if the dog is breathing and has a heartbeat. If the dog is not breathing and has no heartbeat or pulse, begin CPR.
2. If the dog is unconscious, check to be sure that the airway is open.
3. Pull out the tongue to keep the airway clear.
4. Control any bleeding (see chapter 8) and transport the animal to a veterinarian.

SHOCK

dures: If the injury does not require CPR, follow these proce-
1. Calm your dog and speak soothingly.
2. Let the dog assume the most comfortable position that causes the least pain.
3. When possible, splint or otherwise support broken bones before moving the dog.
4. Cover your dog with a coat or blanket. Do not wrap tightly.
5. Transport large dogs on a flat surface or in a hammock stretcher. Carry small dogs, being careful to protect any injured areas.
6. Muzzle the dog only if you feel there is a chance it might bite you.
7. Always take your dog to a veterinary hospital immediately if you suspect they may be in shock.

CHAPTER 8
INJURIES AND BLEEDING

Your dog is determined to explore the world, running and playing, often with no sense of danger. This can sometimes lead to injuries. The good news is that you can treat many minor wounds as long as you have a little bit of knowledge and a good first-aid kit. Remember, having a complete first-aid kit ready when you need it will give you peace of mind, as well as a head start when situations requiring medical care arise. I cannot stress strongly enough the need to have a well-stocked first-aid kit prepared for your pet.

INJURIES AND BLEEDING

There are a variety of types of wounds your dog could receive that could require care, including abrasions, lacerations, bite wounds, punctures, burns, and embedded objects. There are some basic rules when dealing with any wound:

1. Stay calm, and if time allows, grab your first-aid kit.
2. Muzzle the dog for your safety if at any time you feel the dog may be in pain.
3. While there is a very low risk of transmitting infection between humans and dogs, the use of nonlatex disposable gloves is still recommended when treating wounds to help keep the wound clean.

    If you have time, clip away the hair around the dog's injury. Be sure to use only blunt-tipped scissors. Do not cut too close to the skin and be sure to keep the scissors parallel to the dog's body so that you'll be less likely to poke the skin if your dog moves suddenly.
4. Trim away the hair, starting at the injury itself and working outward. This will let you take a closer look at the wound so that you can evaluate how severe it is.

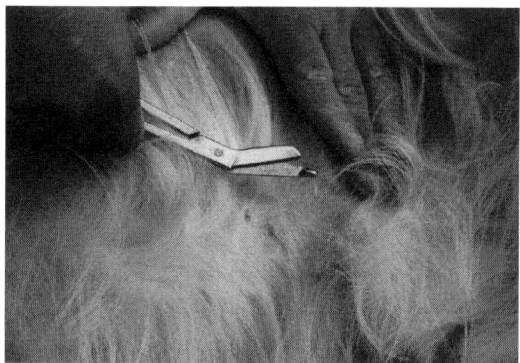

Always use blunt-tipped scissors or clippers to avoid causing any injury to the dog.

5. Clean the injured area. Dog wounds can easily become infected, especially if the injury is a puncture wound, such as a bite. Irrigate the wound with an antiseptic solution such as Betadine, a 3 percent hydrogen peroxide solution, or an antibacterial cleanser. If you don't have any of these handy, a sterile saline solution is also fine. (Add one teaspoon of salt to one quart of warm water to make your own saline solution.) The best way to irrigate the wound is to fill a disposable syringe (the kind the veterinarian gives you to dispense liquid medications, for example) with the cleansing liquid, and flush out the injury several times. Repeat until the area looks clean and there doesn't appear to be any debris left in the wound.

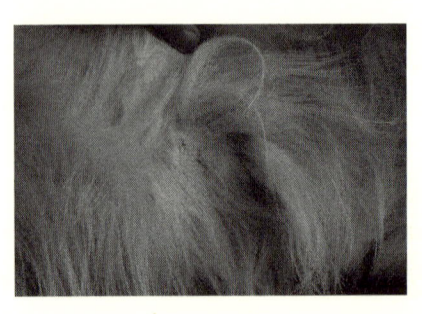

Any wound larger than half an inch will require stitches.

6. Pat the injured area dry. Using a slightly damp sterile gauze pad, apply some antiseptic ointment. Avoid using a dry pad for this task, as it may stick to the wound. If the cut is on an area that your dog can easily lick, don't use too much ointment, as they will probably lick it right off!
7. Keep an eye on the wound for several days. Keep the area clean and watch for any swelling, tenderness, or redness that could indicate infection. If you're in any doubt that the wound is healing well, call your veterinarian immediately. Any laceration (cut) over half an inch long will require stitches.

INJURIES AND BLEEDING

Major wounds are a little trickier. In some cases, you may need to provide emergency treatment and then immediately transport the dog to a veterinarian, as he may need stitches, surgery, medication, etc. What kinds of injuries require immediate veterinary attention?

Any wound involving heavy bleeding. Heavy bleeding is defined as heavily oozing or spurting bright red blood. When there is bleeding of this sort, it is imperative that you apply direct pressure. This is a life-threatening condition. Losing more than 1/5 of her total blood volume will cause the dog to go into shock. As a general rule, an eighty-pound dog has about 2.5 to 3.0 liters of blood. Any loss of blood over 20 percent, which for an average-size dog is only .5 liters of blood, can cause shock. By way of comparison, that's less liquid than what is in two cans of pop. Obviously, this amount will be much less in smaller dogs. With this kind of bleeding, you will probably not have time to grab your first-aid kit. (Controlling bleeding is covered in more detail later in this chapter.)

Any injury involving possible broken bones or internal injuries. These kinds of injuries are likely if your dog has been hit by a car, for example. You can often determine that your dog has a broken bone or internal injuries by how he is acting. Is he walking normally? Is he favoring a certain part of his body? Is he avoiding putting weight on one of his legs? Broken bones can be quite painful, so your dog may also be whining. You might also be able to see some deformity or other sign of injury at the fracture site. This can be quite disturbing to see, but you must take action and splint the fracture. (Splinting is covered in more detail later in this chapter.)

Animal bites. If your dog suffers a bite injury, the resulting puncture wound can be quite serious. The first concern is the location of the bite. If a large mastiff is bit on the leg by a small poodle, there might be minor bleeding and some damage to the structure under the skin. Such an injury is not life threatening. However, if a mastiff bites a poodle and the puncture wounds are across the chest or stomach, the danger can be enormous. Injuries to a dog's lungs, heart, liver, and spleen can be fatal. Dogs with large, wide jaws can exert a great deal of pressure when they bite. As a rule of thumb, the wider the head, the more pressure the animal can exert and the more potential there is for serious injury should the dog bite.

Another serious risk related to any animal bite is rabies. Rabies is a deadly viral infection that is mainly spread by infected animals. Rabies is spread by infected saliva entering the body through a bite or broken skin. The virus travels from the wound to the brain, where it causes swelling, or inflammation. This inflammation causes the symptoms of the disease.

Most rabies deaths occur in human children. In the past, dog bites caused most human cases of rabies in the United States. But in recent years, more cases of human rabies have been linked to bats and raccoons. Although dog bites are a common cause of rabies in developing countries, there have been no reports of rabies caused by dog bites in the United States for a number of years due to widespread animal vaccination. Other wild animals that can spread the rabies virus include foxes and skunks.

The actual time between infection with rabies and when you get sick (called the incubation period) ranges anywhere from ten days to seven years. The average incubation period is three to seven weeks. Symptoms of rabies may include:

- Anxiety, stress, and tension
- Drooling
- Convulsions
- Exaggerated sensation at the bite site
- Excitability
- Loss of feeling in one or more areas of the body

INJURIES AND BLEEDING

- Loss of muscle function
- Low-grade fever (102°F or lower)
- Muscle spasms
- Numbness and tingling
- Pain at the site of the bite
- Restlessness
- Difficulty drinking (which can cause spasms of the voice box)

If an animal bites you, try to gather as much information about the animal as possible. Call your local animal control authorities to safely capture the animal. If rabies is suspected, the animal will be watched for signs of infection. A special test called immunofluorescence is also used to look at the brain tissue of dead animals when there is a suspicion that they may have carried rabies The same test can be used to check for rabies in humans using a piece of skin from the neck. Doctors can also look for the rabies virus in saliva and spinal fluid, although these tests are not as sensitive and may need to be repeated.

If there is any risk of rabies, the patient will be given a series of preventive vaccines. These are generally given in five doses over twenty-eight days. Most patients also receive a treatment called human rabies immunoglobulin (HRIG). This is given the day the bite occurs.

Go to the emergency room or call your local emergency number (such as 911) if any animal bites you. Call your doctor right away if you are exposed to animals that can carry rabies, such as bats, foxes, and skunks. Call even if no bite took place. Immunization and treatment for possible rabies exposure is recommended for up to fourteen days after an exposure or bite.

Follow these precautions to help prevent rabies:
- Avoid contact with animals you don't know.
- Get vaccinated if you work in a high-risk occupation or travel to countries with a high rate of rabies.

- Make sure your pets receive the proper immunizations. Dogs and cats should get rabies vaccines by four months of age, followed by a booster shot one year later, and another one every one or three years, depending on the type of vaccine used.

Controlling Bleeding

In the event of a serious injury, you may need to know how to control bleeding. The first thing you need to understand is that there are two types of bleeding. The good news is that it is usually possible to control bleeding regardless of the type of bleeding with which you are dealing.

The first type of bleeding is oozing. Think of this type of bleeding as being similar to a bloody nose. There is blood flow, but blood loss is not happening quickly.

The second and more critical type of bleeding is arterial bleeding, which is when bleeding is coming from an artery. With this type of bleeding, you may see blood squirting or spurting from the injury. This squirting blood (which is sometimes called blood spurt, blood spray, blood gush, or blood jet) is what happens when a large blood vessel such as an artery is cut. Blood pressure causes the blood to spray out of the wound at a rapid but intermittent rate coinciding with the beating of the heart. As the heart squeezes, there is pressure applied to the arteries to move the blood. This rapid, copious blood loss can lead to death.

The first thing to do when faced with a major wound on a dog is often to stop the bleeding as quickly as possible. You can usually do this by placing a sterile gauze pad over the dog's wound and applying constant, firm pressure.

INJURIES AND BLEEDING

Place a gauze pad over the wound.

Keep the pressure constant. Don't lift the pad to see if the bleeding has slowed or replace the pad when it becomes soaked. Both of these actions will interfere with the blood-clotting effect that you're trying to achieve. If the pad does become soaked with blood, just add another one on top of it. It can be difficult to resist the urge to check the wound. A good rule of thumb is to hold the gauze in place for about seven minutes.

If the wound is still bleeding after that amount of time has passed, you must apply more pressure with greater force. To do this you may need to apply a pressure bandage. This can be accomplished by wrapping your dog's wound with Kerlix and tightening the gauze until it applies pressure to the site. You can use vet wrap but you must use caution as you can apply the vet wrap to tight and cut off circulation to the extremity and or cause tendon damage. Anytime you are wrapping a lower leg with vet wrap you must apply a padding layer evenly on the entire leg. Be careful not to tighten the pressure bandage too tightly if you are wrapping the chest area, If you have ever had a broken arm the cotton pre cast wrap works well. The vet wrap must not be left on for a long period of time and it may tighten up if it gets wet. Be sure to wrap quite a bit above and below the wound. Vet wrap should never be used wrapped around the head or around the chest area as the chest needs to be able to expand in order for the dog to take in a full breath. Once you have controlled the bleeding using this technique, proceed to the veterinarian.

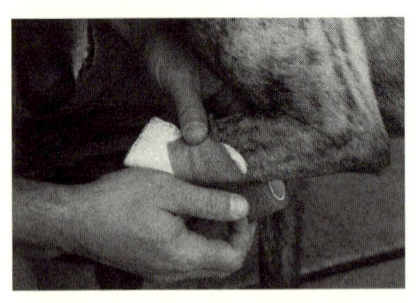

For a wound on a leg, begin to wrap the leg with the gauze pad in place.

If applying a pressure bandage does not control the bleeding, you can attempt to apply pressure to the dog's major arteries. The major arteries are found inside and above the front legs (in the dog's "armpits"), inside and above the hind legs, and under the tail. This is best accomplished by wrapping your hands high around the affected extremity and squeezing.

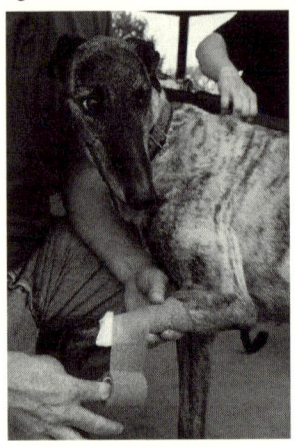

Wrap the entire leg as you go.

INJURIES AND BLEEDING

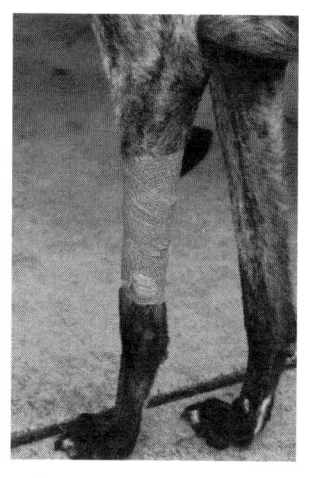

Get your dog to the veterinarian as quickly as possible after completing the wrap.

If both using a pressure bandage and applying pressure to the dog's major arteries fail to stop the bleeding, you can try one last resort: a tourniquet. Tourniquets should be used as a last resort only when other methods for controlling bleeding have failed. Using a tourniquet can have long-term consequences. If your dog survives her injury, there is a good chance that she will lose her leg. This is because applying a tourniquet cuts off all blood supply and circulation to the area below the tourniquet. Can a dog live a healthy, happy life with three legs? *Yes!* I personally would rather have a happy, healthy, three-legged dog than a deceased four-legged one.

To apply a tourniquet, you will need to use Kerlix to tie a knot around the leg above the wound. Next, place a hard object (such as a thick stick or screwdriver) on top of the knot. Tie another knot on top of the object. Twist the object to tighten the tourniquet around the leg. Continue to tighten the tourniquet until the bleeding stops, and then tie the object in place.

K9 MEDIC

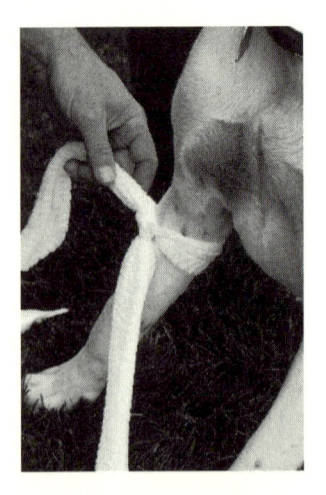

Tie a knot above the wound, being careful never to tie it over a joint.

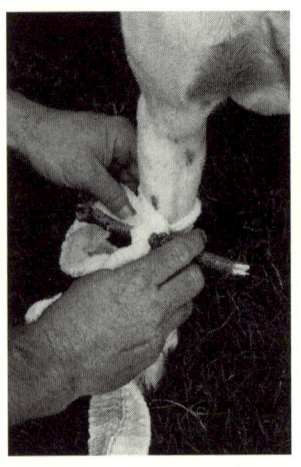

A stick can work nicely for this procedure, as long as it is strong enough.

INJURIES AND BLEEDING

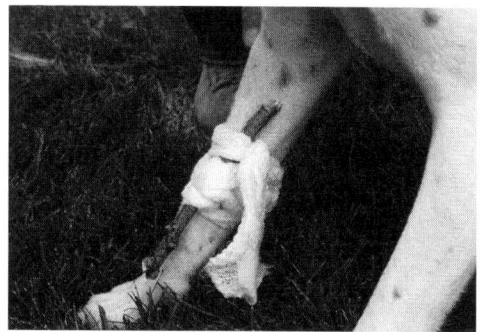

Once you have stopped the bleeding, wrap the stick with the Kerlix and tie a knot to prevent the tourniquet from loosening.

Types of Bleeding Wounds and How to Treat Them

Abrasions are scrapes to the skin's top layers. When it comes to an abrasion, I always think of a softball player sliding into second base who scrapes his leg. That is an abrasion. Shallow abrasions tend to heal easily, while larger ones can be more serious.

To care for an abrasion, first wash your hands and put on disposable gloves, if possible. Apply a sterile, water-soluble (non-petroleum-based) lubricant so the dog's hair does not contaminate the wound while you shave the area. Gently clip the hair around the area.

Flush the wound with warm water or saline solution. (Again, add one teaspoon of salt to one quart of warm water to make your own saline solution.) Then wash the wound with water or saline solution to remove any remaining dirt or debris. If necessary, wet a gauze sponge with sterile saline solution to gently clean away any remaining debris.

Take your dog to the veterinarian for treatment if the abrasion is larger than a quarter, seems painful, is red, does not begin to heal after two to three days, oozes a yellow or foul-smelling discharge, or if you are unsure of its depth or severity.

Lacerations are wounds that cut through the skin to the deeper, underlying tissue layers. They can be deep enough to involve underlying veins, arteries, nerves, ligaments, muscles, tendons, or even bone. It is crucial to assess your dog's condition and the extent of the laceration so you can treat it correctly. Lacerations that are larger than half an inch should be evaluated by a veterinarian. If the laceration is minor, you can treat it at home using the treatment described above for abrasions.

Burns

It is important to take burn injuries seriously. The skin is the largest organ of the body. Injuries to the skin, including burns, can have devastating health effects. Burns affecting as little as 15 percent of the body's surface area can be fatal.

Most information regarding burn care and healing for dogs is extrapolated from human medicine. In recent years, huge advances in human burn care have proven beneficial for pets as well.

Burn severity is classified based on how deep the burn is and the extent of the body burned. There are three types of burns:

1. Superficial partial thickness burns (which are similar to first-degree burns in humans). Symptoms of these injuries include reddening of the skin, pain, and swelling.
2. Deep partial thickness burns (which are similar to second-degree burns in humans). Symptoms of these injuries include blisters, redness, pain, and swelling.
3. Full thickness burns (which are similar to third-degree burns in humans). Symptoms of these injuries include swelling under the skin, loss of skin, and an absence of pain.

INJURIES AND BLEEDING

All burns are serious and should be considered emergencies. Obviously, full thickness burns are the most serious kind of burn your dog can suffer; however, more minor burns should also be treated seriously. A superficial burn over 50 percent of the body has the possibility to cause much greater injury and illness than a full thickness burn involving only 3 percent of the body.

When dealing with a dog that has suffered a burn injury, you will want to assess the following:
- What caused the burn?
- How long ago did the burn occur?
- What treatments have already been given?
- For what length of time was the dog exposed to the hot item?
- Is there any missing hair?
- Do you see any red skin or blisters?

Prompt veterinary attention is crucial to a positive outcome when it comes to burns. If your dog has been burned, he may be susceptible to infection, dehydration, and shock. Your veterinarian will perform a thorough physical examination to determine the proper course of treatment.

It may be very tempting to rapidly cool your burned pet with ice or ice packs, but don't do it. Ice and ice packs can result in overcooling, low body temperature, and, at worst, frostbite or even death. A dog's normal temperature is between 100°F and 102.5°F. If you overcool the animal, you may cause hypothermia.

The treatment of burns is based on the depth of the burn. Minor burns (also known as superficial or partial thickness burns), which usually involve less than 10 percent of the body, can respond well to cleaning the wound and using topical antibiotic creams. However, be sure to confirm with your veterinarian that this course of action is appropriate.

Deep (or partial thickness) burns, which involve more than 15 percent of the body, need more significant treatment. If there are no blisters and the skin is intact, you can apply a piece of cool gauze to the wound and then transport the dog to the veterinarian. However, if the skin has oozing, broken blisters, simply place a piece of dry gauze on the wound before taking the dog to receive medical attention. Do *not* attempt to cool the dog.

The deepest burns (full thickness burns) require extensive, prolonged treatment that can be quite expensive. Even with the best of care, these kinds of injuries are often fatal. Expect your veterinarian to discuss the severity of the situation and the chances of long-term recovery for your pet, as well as costs. Sadly, many owners of pets who have suffered extensive full thickness burns choose euthanasia because the cost of treatment is very high and recovery is often unlikely.

It is important to remember that there is no true veterinarian-approved home care for most burns. In the past, people applied butter to burns. This in turn held the heat of the injury in, causing more damage. This is the last thing you want to do. When it comes to burn care, stick with the basic treatment recommended by your dog's medical provider and do not use home remedies.

Many burns are true accidents that cannot be prevented. However, there are some things you can do to reduce the risk of your pet suffering a burn. Do not allow your dog to roam unsupervised. Be sure to keep your dog out of harm's way when using a barbecue or grill, and keep your pet away from all hot items and any situations where a burn could occur.

Insect Bites

Dogs are susceptible to spider bites and bee stings. Insects often sting the soft, less-hairy areas of your pet, such as the nose and feet.

INJURIES AND BLEEDING

These bites can sometimes cause allergic reactions, difficulty breathing, pain, itching, and licking at the site. There may be redness, discoloration, or hives (bumps in the skin) around the site, which can sometimes spread to other body parts

It is important to be aware that a rare, severe allergic reaction to an insect bite can lead to anaphylactic shock. This can occur within a few minutes of the bite, or progressively over several hours. Anaphylactic shock is a profound physical reaction that can quickly lead to unconsciousness and even death.

If your dog's face and neck are swollen, check his airway, breathing, and circulation. If your dog's breathing is noisy or labored, take him to a veterinarian immediately. Check for signs of shock. Examine the injury to see if the stinger is still present; insect stingers are usually black and very small. Do not attempt to pick it out, as this can release more toxin. Instead, scrape it off with a firm object, such as your fingernail or a credit card. Then apply a cold compress or ice packs wrapped in a towel to help control swelling. If possible, you may want to give the dog a dose of antihistamine (see dosing information below). Transport your dog to a veterinary hospital immediately.

Many over-the-counter products, including Benadryl˚, contain the antihistamine diphenhydramine *along with* other cold or allergy medications (i.e., acetaminophen or pseudoephedrine). It is extremely important to ensure that the product you give your dog contains *only* diphenhydramine. It is also extremely important to give the dog oral medication *only* if she is conscious, able to breathe, and not vomiting.

The antihistamine dosage for a dog is found below.
- Small dogs (less than thirty pounds): ten milligrams.
- Medium-sized dogs (thirty to fifty pounds): twenty-five milligrams.

- Large and very large dogs (greater than fifty pounds): fifty milligrams.
- Never give a dog more than fifty milligrams of diphenhydramine.

Tail Swelling and Other Tail Injuries

While tail injuries or swelling are generally not life-threatening emergencies, these common injuries can be painful to your pet. The signs and symptoms of such an injury include blood on the tail, holding the tail awkwardly, and licking or biting the tail. The most common causes of such injuries include abscesses or other wounds, excessive exercise or swimming, and trauma (getting the tail caught in a door, for example).

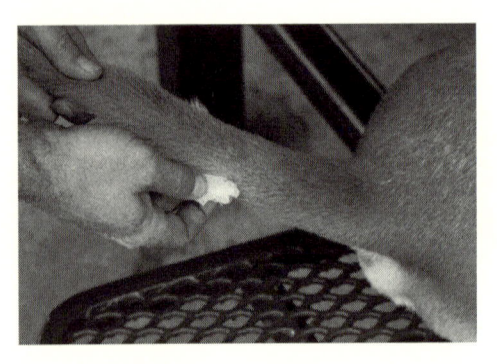

Clean the wound and then hold gauze over the injured area.

To treat these injuries, first gently examine the area to see if it's red and inflamed. Control any bleeding with a four-inch square piece of gauze. Once bleeding has stopped, bandage the wound. To perform this procedure, first place the gauze square over the wound. Then wrap the entire tail with the pre cast wrap. Then take vet wrap starting on the under- side of the base of the tail, pull the vet wrap all the way to the tip of the tail then back up the top side of the tail. Then continue back down the

INJURIES AND BLEEDING

tail until you reach the base. Wrap the tail with the vet wrap end over end, moving back to the tip of the tail. This will give you a wrap that will control bleeding and protect the tail from further injury. Take your dog to your veterinarian, who may decide to take an X-ray to rule out a bone fracture.

Place a piece of the cotton over the wound.

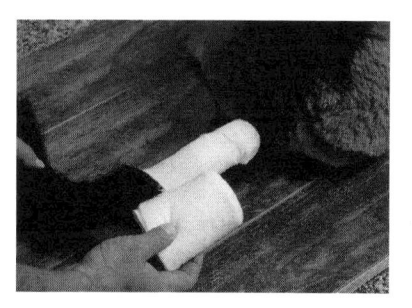

Wrap the entire tail with cotton tightly.

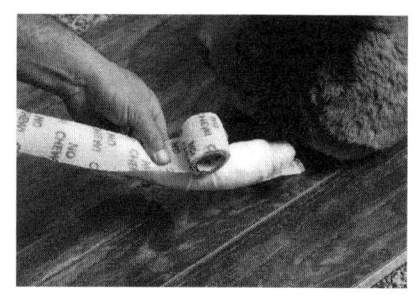

Place vet wrap on top and bottom of the tail.

Wrap the entire tail with vet wrap to the tip.

Embedded Objects

You can try to remove a foreign object embedded in your dog's skin as long as it does not appear to penetrate into the deep tissues. It is essential not to push the object deeper into the animal. You should then contact your veterinarian to determine when the wound should be evaluated.

If the object appears deeply embedded, do not attempt to remove it. It is best to add padding around the object so it does not move and cause more injury. Take the dog to a veterinarian as soon as possible; she may need immediate surgery or intervention once the object is removed.

Signs and symptoms of an embedded object may include bleeding; evidence of an infection (redness, swelling, discharge, or pain); and bruising. Keep in mind that embedded foreign objects can cause significant internal injuries to both muscles and internal organs.

Bite Wounds

It can be quite scary to witness your dog engaged in a fight, and dogfights are also extremely dangerous. *Never* attempt to break up

INJURIES AND BLEEDING

a dogfight yourself, as the risk of being bitten is quite high. Remember, your safety should always come first. Never put your body between two dogs (or allow anyone else to do so).

To treat any animal bite wound, clean the wound well with soap and water and then seek professional medical help. You'll need a doctor to thoroughly clean the wound and remove any foreign objects. Stitches may not always be necessary for animal bite wounds, but this is a decision best left to a veterinarian.

If a bite wound is not immediately treated, the injured dog may develop an infection or abscess one or two days after being bitten. An abscess is a soft swelling around the wound. The top of the swelling may be red or blue. Abscesses can be quite painful. When ruptured, pus will be visible and a foul odor will generally be present. Signs of bite wound infection include fever (usually above 103°F), lethargy, loss of appetite, and pain when the affected area is touched.

Ear Bleeding

Ear problems are quite common in dogs, especially those with long, floppy ears such as basset hounds and cocker spaniels. Most of these issues are quite harmless and can easily be treated at home. However, severe infections can lead to hearing loss, so it's best to have your dog seen by a veterinarian even if the issue seems minor.

For a bleeding ear, apply direct pressure to the bleeding site with a cloth or piece of gauze for five minutes. If bleeding absolutely will not stop with pressure alone, a head bandage may be used.

To make a head bandage, place a gauze sponge or other piece of clean cloth over the wound. Hold the ear away from the head and place a piece of gauze directly behind the ear. You will end up folding the ear back onto the top of the dogs head. If you do not place the bandage behind the ear there is a chance blood flow to the ear may be cut of causing a tourniquet effect. Wrap with Kerlix, starting from the tip of the ear and wrapping in a downward fashion. Some veterinarians like to leave the unaffected ear out of the wrap and some feel there is some benefit to wrapping both ears in the wrap to provide some comfort. Once you reach the base of the ear, continue around the side of the head. Come around the jaw to the other side of the face and head. Repeat two or three times. Finally, tape down the Kerlix.

Make sure that you can place two fingers inside the bandage to ensure that it is not too tight. Wrapping a head bandage too tightly may make it difficult for your dog to breathe. Watch your dog closely to make sure there are no breathing difficulties. Take your dog to the veterinarian immediately to see if sutures are needed.

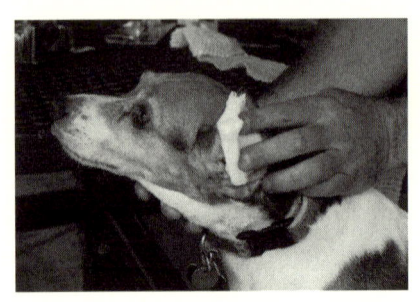

Hold the gauze in place and wrap the ear back against the head.

INJURIES AND BLEEDING

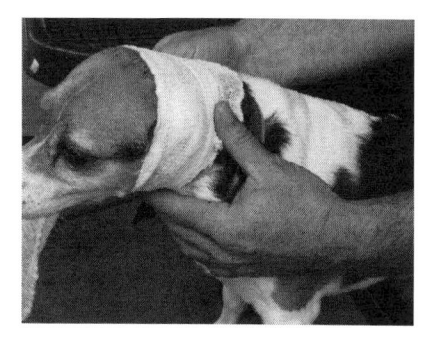

Be careful to avoid wrapping too tightly, as this may make it difficult for the dog to breathe.

Off to the vet we go.

CHAPTER 9
PAD WOUNDS

The pads of your dog's feet contain many blood vessels that cause them to bleed heavily when injured. And unfortunately, due to their location and function, pad injuries are quite common.

To treat pad wounds, first check the scene for safety. Put on nonlatex disposable gloves, if possible.

Pad injuries can be tricky. Best practice would be to remove the object so it does not get pressed deeper if the dog puts pressure on the foot. Another good option would be to carry the dog after the dressing is applied to prevent further injury. However, you must use caution when taking this step. This could be painful for the dog and

PAD WOUNDS

you must apply a muzzle to reduce the rick to yourself. Removing foreign objects embedded in the pad will increase bleeding, so you must have your first-aid kit ready as well. A dog's pads can bleed a great deal, so dealing with such wounds can become quite messy. It is best to limit the dog's activity while you treat him, as you do not want him to put weight on the affected area and push any foreign objects deeper into the skin.

Wash the area with saline solution or warm water. Dry the injured foot. Bandage the injury by first placing a four-inch gauze square over the wound. If you have the cast padding you can tear several pieces and place them between all the webbing of the dogs pads. You can then wrap the entire foot with the pre cast wrap. You will then want to place to outer layer over the pre cast wrapping. If you do choose to use vet wrap just be cautious as if wrapped to tight it can cause a lack of circulation. If you do not have pre cast wrapping you my also use Kerlix. You can place the Kerlix between the dogs pads, then wrap the entire foot and leg. You may secure the Kerlix with some tape.

Wrap the bandage between the dog's claws.

Make sure the bandage is not too tight. Check for toe swelling and feel the limb just above the bandage for any coolness, pain, or swelling. If any of these are evident, loosen the bandage. After bandaging, take the dog to the veterinarian to assess whether any further treatment is necessary.

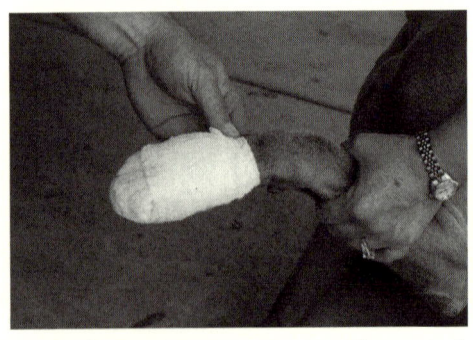

You may then use vet wrap to wrap the entire leg.

CHAPTER 10
SEIZURES

Unfortunately, seizures are very common in dogs. Idiopathic epilepsy, the single most common canine seizure disorder, is reported to occur in anywhere from 0.5 to 5.7 percent of all dogs.

What is a seizure? Regardless of the terminology used (seizure, convulsion, fit, or epilepsy), a seizure is what happens when a sudden and uncontrolled burst of neurological activity occurs in the brain. Sometimes the disturbance remains localized in a small area, such as the face or one limb. This is called a focal motor seizure. Usually, however, the uncontrolled firing of neurons spreads from the brain throughout the body, causing generalized, full-body convulsions.

Seizures are sometimes difficult to recognize, and no two look exactly alike. The typical seizure, however, might proceed as follows:

1. The dog becomes nervous or agitated, sensing that something abnormal is about to happen. Some dogs seek out their owners when they sense a seizure approaching, looking for help and reassurance. This is called the pre-ictal period.
2. The dog begins to tremble. His eyes glaze over and he loses touch with his environment, appears blind, and does not respond to his owner's voice or touch.
3. Trembling becomes more severe and the dog becomes stiff. The dog falls, usually on his side, and begins to paddle his legs and convulse, sometimes violently. The dog might clench his teeth or chomp his jaws as the seizure progresses. He may whimper or cry. He may also salivate or appear to stop breathing. This stage, known as the ictal stage, usually lasts less than two minutes. The duration of this stage is important because when a seizure lasts more than two minutes, it can become deadly due to a condition called status seizure (which is covered in greater detail later in this chapter).
4. The next stage is called the post-ictal period. The dog begins to recover, but a varying degree of neurological symptoms will usually persist. Commonly, dogs remain "fuzzy" or "foggy" for some time after a seizure. They often pant and seem disoriented. Some dogs sleep for a long period of time following a seizure. The post-ictal stage usually lasts for less than an hour, but can be considerably longer, continuing for up to several days.

SEIZURES

Certain other medical situations look very much like a seizure. Dogs with a disease of the middle ear, the vestibular nerve, or the vestibular nucleus of the brain can show abnormal head position and loss of balance. The onset of symptoms can be quite sudden and is sometimes confused with seizures.

Dogs with cardiac and respiratory diseases can experience fainting episodes that leave them profoundly weak; many may fall abruptly. These dogs might pant rapidly as they try to compensate for poor oxygenation. These behaviors are also often confused with seizures.

Another false alarm is a condition known as reverse sneezing, a common complaint in small dogs. Reverse sneezing is characterized by a rapid series of violent and noisy intakes of breath. Often the chest and abdominal muscles will contract spasmodically during these episodes, which are always self-limiting and are of little medical significance. These incidents are often caused by mild allergic reactions.

Then there are those dogs who twitch or paddle their legs while sleeping. Some will even whimper. This is especially common in young puppies, although many older dogs continue to show these behaviors. This is normal and is usually associated with very deep sleep. Folklore has it that dogs paddling their legs during sleep are dreaming of running through an open field. Who knows? At any rate, it's not a seizure.

The biggest difference between seizures and seizure-like behavior is the dog's state of consciousness. If a dog is exhibiting behaviors that resemble a seizure while conscious, and if the dog is aware of its surroundings or is easily aroused (as in sleep), it is not having a true seizure.

What causes seizures? Unfortunately, it is often impossible to answer that question. I know people who have had a seizure disorder for their entire life without their doctors ever being able to diagnose the cause.

We do know *how* seizures happen, however, even when we don't always know *why*. The normally functioning brain exists in a constantly changing state of balance between bioelectrical impulses. At a certain threshold point, excitatory activity can overwhelm inhibitory influences, leading to a seizure. How close any given animal is to this point (called the seizure threshold) is influenced by a number of factors, including disease, trauma, genetics, toxins, and factors that science has yet to determine. In other words, whether or not an individual dog has a seizure in response to a given stimulus depends on its own particular seizure threshold.

A variety of causes of seizures have been documented in dogs. In some individuals, the cause is metabolic. For example, hypoglycemia (low blood sugar) is a common cause of seizures in toy breed puppies. Hypoglycemia brought on by giving excessive doses of insulin to diabetic dogs, or by insulin-secreting tumors of the pancreas in older dogs, can also cause seizures. Hypocalcaemia (low calcium levels) is another metabolic cause of seizures; this is especially common in postpartum lactating bitches. Hypocalcaemia and hypoglycemia are both thought to be involved in seizures experienced by young puppies with intestinal parasites.

High blood ammonia levels can also lead to seizures. This metabolic disturbance is seen in dogs with liver disease (for example, portosystemic shunts in puppies). Kidney failure and high levels of circulating uremic toxins have also been known to cause seizures, although this is less common.

When a dog that has never had seizure problems before has a seizure that manifests suddenly, the cause is often ingestion of something toxic. In other words, if your dog has a seizure and has never had one before, think poison.

SEIZURES

Seizures are sometimes caused by inflammation of the central nervous system (CNS), also known as encephalitis. There are many significant infectious causes of encephalitis in dogs. Canine distemper, for example, is one of the most common causes of seizures in puppies.

Heat stroke is another all-too-familiar cause of seizures and death in dogs. Everyone knows heat stroke can happen when an animal is left unattended in an automobile on a warm day, with or without the windows open. And anyone who frequents outdoor dog shows in hot weather has heard horror stories of dogs overcome by excessive heat outside, particularly breeds with heavy coats.

Trauma to the head can lead to seizures if there is hemorrhaging or swelling of the brain or surrounding tissues or subsequent formation of scar tissue or blood clots. Many dog owners are stunned to learn that it is not uncommon for seizures to result from a traumatic episode that occurred years earlier. Bleeding and swelling can also be caused by tumors or surrounding structures. Tumors are most common in older dogs.

The cause of the most common form of seizures in dogs, known as idiopathic epilepsy, remains unknown. This is also true in humans. Although the term *idiopathic* means "self-originated," it's really just a technical way of saying the cause of the disease is unknown. Even though a large percentage of seizures are diagnosed as idiopathic, testing for other possible causes should always be performed, especially if the seizures are severe, frequent, or occur in clusters.

How are the causes of seizures diagnosed? The initial workup of a patient with seizures includes a thorough physical examination, a meticulous medical history, and blood and urine tests. A complete blood count can reveal signs of infection or inflammation. A chemistry profile can reveal metabolic causes of seizures by testing for biochemical markers of liver, kidney, glucose, and electrolyte disturbances. Changes in the urine can also reflect kidney, liver, or other metabolic abnormalities. Blood samples can also reveal toxic levels of lead, another possible cause of seizures.

If an obvious cause of the seizures isn't discovered through initial testing, further tests can sometimes prove useful. An important element in the clinical evaluation of just about any patient with a central nervous system disorder is the analysis of cerebrospinal fluid (CSF). Changes in CSF protein concentration, blood cell population, and CSF pressure can indicate specific diseases of the central nervous system.

To perform these tests, CSF is collected while the dog is under general anesthesia. The dog is positioned on her side. An area at the base of the skull and upper neck is clipped and surgically scrubbed. Once the head is positioned correctly, a needle is carefully placed into the space between the base of the skull and the first cervical vertebra. CSF is then collected through the needle and submitted to a laboratory for analysis. To measure CSF pressure, an instrument called a manometer is attached to the needle. This measurement is important because pressure is often elevated in the case of issues such as brain tumors, for example.

While the patient is anesthetized, an electroencephalogram (EEG) can also be performed. EEG equipment is usually found only at teaching hospitals or large referral centers, which is unfortunate because this test can yield useful information. To perform an EEG, small wire electrodes are placed on the dog's skin at various points overlying the brain. The electrical activity of the brain can then be observed. The electrode's pins do penetrate the dog's skin, but they are very small and the slight injuries they cause are not traumatic. In fact, EEGs can even be performed on conscious dogs. This test is simple and risk-free; the methodology is very similar to an EKG test of the heart. But interpretation of the results usually requires the services of a neurological specialist.

The last diagnostic option available to investigate seizures is a brain scan. Computerized tomography (what is known as a CT scan) and magnetic resonance imaging (MRI) are just beginning to be available in veterinary medicine. These diagnostic imaging techniques yield a wealth of information and can be very sensitive indicators of structural central nervous system diseases. However, as with all other tests, these scans are negative in cases of idiopathic epilepsy. Brain scans also require the use of general anesthesia. These procedures are usually quite expensive, which is why very few dogs are tested to this extent.

If the underlying cause of a dog's seizure disorder is identified, treatment can be directed at correcting the abnormality or eliminating the cause. Even if an underlying cause is found, however, anticonvulsant drugs are generally needed to control seizures. This is also true in the case of dogs with idiopathic epilepsy. Owners should realize that seizures are rarely eliminated completely. The goal of therapy is to reduce the frequency and severity of seizures to a level that the dog and his family can live with.

Dog owners need to be aware that in some serious cases, seizure conditions can literally change a dog's personality. The dog may become vicious, attempting to bite anyone around, including children. Sadly, some of these dogs have to be euthanized.

Seizures are almost never fatal on their own. The key word here is *almost*. When seizures last for longer than two minutes, they can develop into a condition called status epilepticus, which is characterized by continuous, uncontrollable seizure activity. This can lead to exhaustion, hypoglycemia, hyperthermia, oxygen depletion, brain damage, and, eventually, death. Status epilepticus is an extreme emergency that requires immediate veterinary treatment.

If a young puppy or a lactating bitch has a seizure, have her seen by a veterinarian immediately. A single isolated seizure in an otherwise healthy adult dog, however, does not usually require emergency veterinary care, although an appointment should be scheduled promptly for a thorough workup. If a dog has multiple seizures in one day, emergency care should be sought immediately.

All of this technical detail aside, what should you do if your dog has a seizure?

1. Watching a dog have a seizure is terrifying, especially if it's a dog you love. First and foremost, when a dog has a seizure, it is important for owners to remain calm—no matter how difficult that may be.
2. The dog should be moved to a safe place or laid on a rug to minimize the chances of injury.
3. If possible, time the length of the seizure. Observe the dog carefully so that you can give the veterinarian a clear and accurate account of the event. This often proves to be of great importance when visiting the veterinarian, especially if the dog is on any medication. The vet will be able to look at the dog's current medication and perhaps make some adjustments.
4. Dogs do not swallow their tongues during seizures, so owners do not need to take any action to prevent that issue. Never put your hands near a seizing dog's mouth.
5. Many veterinarians believe that the length and severity of the post-ictal phase after a seizure can be decreased by gently trying to calm and soothe the dog. Panicking certainly won't help!
6. Never sit down with a injured animal. When they are in an altered state of mind often their actions can be un predictable. Your safety must always come first.

7. Film the Seizure with your smart phone. I know this sounds somewhat crazy but when you are able to lm the events it will help your veterinarian diagnose potential problem. It will also keep accurate time of the incident.

DANGER: When a dog is coming out of a seizure they may not be aware of their surroundings and might be very frightened. There is a good chance they may bite or be aggressive. Your safety must always come first.

CHAPTER 11
SPRAINS, STRAINS, FRACTURES AND DISLOCATIONS

I am often asked what the difference is between a sprain, a strain, and a fracture. A sprain is an injury involving a ligament (the tissue that connects bones to bones or bones to muscles). A strain is an injury to a muscle. A fracture is an injury to a bone. But for our purposes, the technical details don't really matter, as we are going to treat these injuries in very much the same way. The difference will come once your veterinarian has looked at the X-rays and proceeds to determine the best treatment for your dog.

SPRAINS, STRAINS, FRACTURES AND DISLOCATIONS

What are the signs and symptoms of a sprain or strain?
1. Limping (not placing the limb down at all or placing less weight on it)
2. Pain when the area is touched
3. Crying when walking, or refusing to walk
4. Swelling

If your dog is suffering from a sprain or strain, you will probably not be able to tell exactly what is wrong. You must restrict the dog's activity and then splint the leg. (Splinting is covered in greater detail later in this chapter.)

Fractures are breaks in the bone. When a dog has a broken bone, it can be quite painful. It is wise to muzzle a dog before attempting to splint a fracture.

Signs and symptoms of a fracture include:
1. Disfigurement (part of the limb may seem to be positioned abnormally). I know this sounds gruesome and, to be honest, it is. This is when composure and quick action are crucial
2. Lameness (not placing full weight on the limb)
3. Pain
4. Deformity under the skin (bones can be completely broken without breaking the dog's skin)
5. Part of the bone sticking through the skin
6. Possible bruising (which can be difficult to see under the fur)
7. Swelling

We are going to treat sprains, strains, and fractures all the same way: with splinting. Splints are used to keep an injury immobilized to prevent further damage. They can be used for injuries at or below the elbow and at or below the knee. To correctly immobilize an injury, the joints above and below the site must be included in the splint. It is important to note that it is not possible to splint the shoulder, although there are procedures that can limit its movement. It is also important to note that I recommend having two people present when attempting to splint an injured dog: one person to hold the broken part and the other person to apply the bandage.

Let's say your dog has broken the bone on the right front leg between the paw and elbow. Once the bone is broken, the leg from the break down is going to be limp, or may even flop around. If the dog is sitting and gets up, the leg will drag, as there is no structure to support it.

Once you have restrained your dog and applied a muzzle, proceed with splinting. Grab your first-aid kit and get out the Kerlix and your splinting material. Use a towel or blanket to wrap and support the limb. For the splint itself, you can use a stick, a piece of wood, cardboard, newspaper, or a magazine rolled around the limb. A wooden dowel would work well, too.

Make sure you have a firm object to use as a splint.

SPRAINS, STRAINS, FRACTURES AND DISLOCATIONS

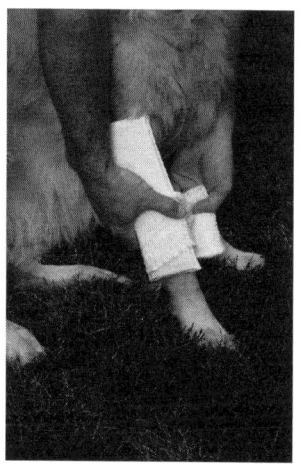

Wrap the leg, being sure to get the joint above and below the injury.

One person is going to hold the leg in place while the other person applies the splint. It is important not to manipulate the broken bone or move the paw at any time, as this could cause a great deal of pain to the dog and could also damage the underlying tissue, causing internal bleeding. When lifting the leg, you must also lift the paw at the same time. Failing to do so will cause movement at the location of the break.

Wrap the Kerlix around the splint. Your goal here is to restrict movement. Once the splint is in place, transport your dog to the veterinarian.

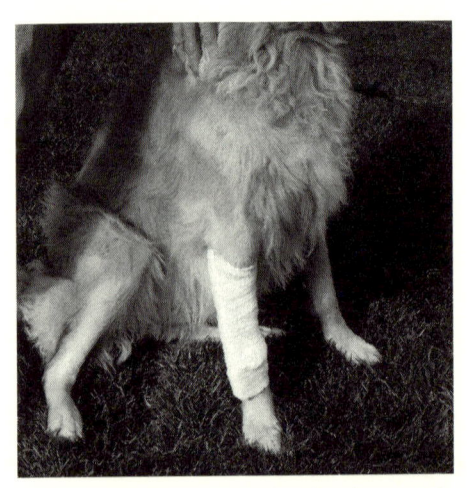

Once you complete the wrap, immediately take your dog to the vet.

The treatment for a broken bone will depend on the severity of the break and the dog's age. Some breaks can be treated with a simple splint or cast, while other breaks require surgery and pins in order to stabilize and repair the break. Some dogs may even require physical rehabilitation. In most cases, younger dogs heal much more quickly than older dogs, and younger dogs usually require casting for a shorter amount of time as well.

Your veterinarian will assess the break through a series of X-rays, as well as checking the dog for any symptoms of shock. Blood tests may also be recommended to ensure the dog is stable enough for surgery and that no other underlying medical conditions or injuries are present.

Follow-up X-rays are needed throughout the healing process to make sure the break is stabilized and healing and to estimate when any cast or splint can be removed.

If a pelvic or rib fracture is suspected, move your dog using a piece of cardboard, a wooden board, or a towel or blanket to keep her from moving during transport to a veterinarian.

SPRAINS, STRAINS, FRACTURES AND DISLOCATIONS

A broken back or neck in a dog is a very serious injury. Your dog may be in extreme pain, so it's very important to carefully muzzle him for your protection. Signs and symptoms of a broken back or neck include:

- Stiff and extended front legs.
- Pain.
- The dog's anus is open.
- The dog may be unable to move his head, hind legs, or both front and hind legs.
- The dog may dribble urine or feces.
- You may see a divot (an area on the spine that appears lower than the rest of the back).

To treat a dog with a possible broken back or neck, try to slide a board under the animal, keeping him as still as possible. To do this, place a board up on its side along the dog's back. It is best to hold the head, chest, and legs to prevent movement. Then lower the board and, at the same time, slide the dog onto it, keeping the body and head as still as possible. Secure your dog to the board by placing tape or torn strips of cloth over him and around the board. Then immediately transport him to a veterinary hospital.

Dislocations

A dislocated bone can be an extremely disturbing sight. The two most common joints that suffer from luxation (complete dislocation) are the hip and the elbow. Congenital disease and trauma can cause an elbow to become luxated. Hip dysplasia is the leading cause of subluxations (partial dislocation) in the hip joint, whereas trauma and hip dysplasia can cause a luxated hip joint. Your dog must see a veterinarian immediately should one of these injuries occur.

Signs and symptoms of a dislocated hip include pain when the area is touched. A dislocated hind leg may appear shorter or longer than the other leg. Also, the foot on a dislocated leg will not reach the ground when the animal stands. A dislocated elbow will appear bent and the foot will not reach the ground. The lower leg will be pointed away from or toward the body in an unnatural-looking way.

In the case of a dislocated elbow, you can attempt to splint the limb in the position in which you find it. Never attempt to place it back in its normal position. This is a job only for your veterinarian.

As a general rule. If your dog is not putting any weight on any of it's legs- the dog should be carried.

For a dislocated hip, transport your dog to a veterinary hospital as soon as possible. The sooner you get them to the hospital, the greater the chances are that the bone can be placed back in the joint without surgery.

CHAPTER 12
BLOAT

Bloat is a very serious health risk for many dogs. Yet many dog owners know very little about it. It is believed to be the second leading killer of dogs after cancer. I myself have lost a dog to bloat, and can tell you that at the time, I knew nothing about it.

There is a great deal of controversy surrounding bloat in dogs. There are many different schools of thought regarding both its causes and prevention. My top priority here is to educate you on the signs and symptoms of bloat and to stress the fact that it can be fatal within *one hour*. I will also give you information on the subject; however, it is crucial that you do your own research before making any decisions regarding bloat prevention. This is one area where I feel you should consult specific breed groups as well as your veterinarian for medical information.

The information in this chapter is not intended to replace advice or guidance from your veterinarian or other pet care professionals. It is simply being shared as an aid to assist you with your own research regarding this very serious problem.

Bloat is an extremely serious condition that should be considered a life-threatening emergency. Dog owners must contact their veterinarian immediately if they suspect that their dog has bloat. If left untreated, bloat is fatal in 95 percent of dogs. Even with treatment, as many as 25 to 33 percent of dogs with bloat die.

There are no home remedies for bloat. That being said some veterinarians may suggest to keep Gas-X or a similar product containing simethicone on hand in case your dog has gas. If you can reduce or slow the gas, you may be able to buy yourself a little more time to get to a vet if your dog is bloating. On the other hand there are veterinarian's who feel simethicone has no direct benefit.

So what exactly is bloat? The technical name for this condition is gastric dilatation volvulus (or GDV). Bloating of the stomach is often related to swallowed air (although food and fluid can also be present). It usually happens when there's an abnormal accumulation of air, fluid, and/or foam in the stomach (gastric dilatation). Stress can be a significant contributing factor as well. Bloat can occur with or without twisting (volvulus) of the stomach.

BLOAT

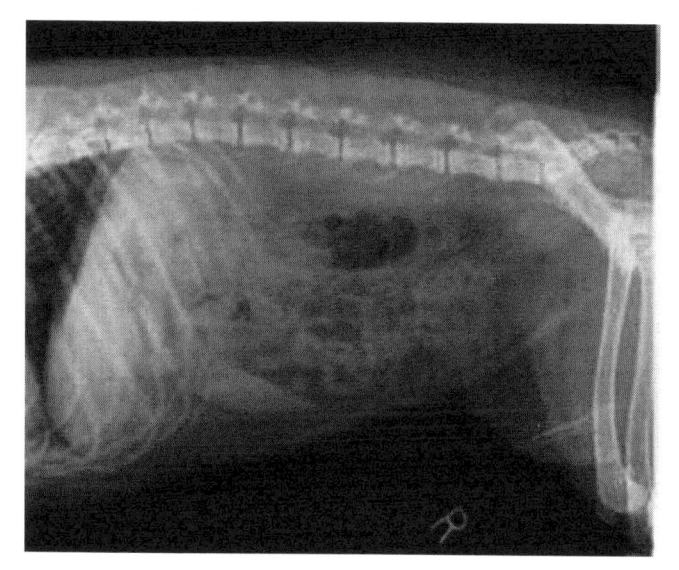

A normal dog stomach.

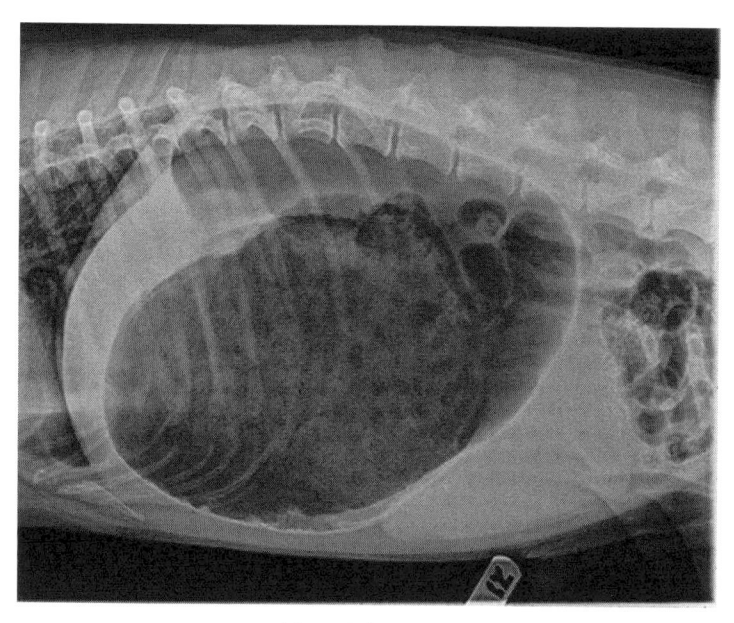

A bloated dog stomach.

As the stomach swells, it may rotate anywhere from 90° to 360°, twisting between its fixed attachments at the esophagus and the duodenum (the upper intestine). The twisting stomach traps air, food, and water inside it. A bloated stomach can obstruct the veins in the abdomen and compresses the vena cava (the vessel that returns blood to the heart), leading to low blood pressure, shock, and damage to internal organs. The combined effects of these problems can quickly kill a dog.

I cannot stress enough that if you believe your dog is experiencing bloat, please get him to a veterinarian immediately! As mentioned previously, bloat can kill in less than an hour, so time is of the essence. Call your veterinarian's office to alert them that you're on your way with a suspected bloat case. It's better to be safe than sorry! The veterinarian will often rush the dog into the CT scan or even the operating room upon your arrival.

Which dogs are vulnerable to bloat? There are a number of factors that seem to affect a dog's vulnerability to this issue. Dogs over seven years of age are more than twice as likely to develop gastric dilatation and volvulus as those who are two to four years of age. It appears that male dogs are twice as likely to develop gastric dilatation and volvulus as females. Dogs fed once a day are twice as likely to develop GDV as those fed twice a day. It appears that dogs who eat rapidly or exercise soon after a meal may also be at increased risk. Temperament also seems to play an important part in bloat risk. Dogs that tend to be more nervous, anxious, or fearful appear to be at an increased risk of developing bloat. Finally, dogs that have bloated before are more prone to bloat again.

There also appears to be a genetic link to this disease. The incidence of bloat is closely correlated to the depth and width of a dog's chest. Several different genes from the parents determine these traits. If both of the dog's parents have particularly deep and narrow chests, it is highly likely that their offspring will have deep and narrow chests as well, along with the resulting problems that may go with it. This appears to be why particular breeds have higher rates of bloat.

Which breeds are most at risk for bloat? While experts disagree, there is some information that is certain. Bloat is much more likely to occur in large breeds with deep, narrow chests. The problem can occur in small dogs as well, but only rarely. The University of Purdue conducted a study of hundreds of dogs that had developed GDV and calculated a ratio of likelihood of a particular breed developing the problem as compared to a mixed-breed dog. For example, using the GDV risk ratio, a Great Dane is 41.4 times more likely to develop GDV than a mixed-breed dog. (The published list of twenty-five breeds and their risk is located at the end of this chapter.)

There are many symptoms of bloat, most of which can also be associated with other health problems or risks. While it is important to be aware of these symptoms, it's perhaps even more important to know your dog well so that you'll be aware when he just isn't acting normally. A dog suffering from bloat will typically exhibit some (but not necessarily all) of the following symptoms:

- Personality changes.
- Attempts to vomit (usually unsuccessful) may occur every five to thirty minutes. This seems to be one of the most common symptoms of bloat, and has been referred to as the "hallmark symptom." Unsuccessful vomiting means either nothing comes up or, possibly, only foam and/or mucous come up.
- Significant anxiety and restlessness, which can be one of the earliest warning signs. The dog may hunch up.
- Lack of normal gurgling and digestive sounds in the abdomen. Many dog owners report this after putting their ear to their dog's belly.

- The abdomen may be tight and drumlike to the touch. You may even be able to see this condition.
- Pale or off-color gums. The gums may be dark red in the early stages of bloat, becoming white or blue in later stages.
- Coughing or unproductive gagging
- Heavy salivating or drooling. This may appear as a foamy mucous around the lips, or as vomit that consists of foamy mucous.
- Unproductive attempts to defecate
- Whining
- Pacing
- Licking the air
- Seeking a hiding place
- Looking at her side or showing other evidence of abdominal pain or discomfort
- Refusal to lie down or even sit down
- Standing spread-legged or bull-legged
- Attempting to stretch out by lengthening the body or going into a praying or crouched position
- Attempting to eat small stones, twigs, and/or grass
- Excessive drinking
- Heavy or rapid panting
- Shallow breathing
- Cold mouth membranes
- Apparent weakness; the dog may be unable to stand or have a spread-legged stance, especially in the advanced stages of bloat.
- Accelerated heartbeat. The heart rate increases as bloating progresses.
- Weak pulse
- Collapse

BLOAT

So how is gastric dilatation and volvulus prevented? Experts disagree regarding this question. Because of the genetic link involved, prospective pet owners should definitely ask breeders if there is a history of GDV in the lineage of any puppy from a high-risk breed. In addition, the following recommendations are sometimes made; although, again, you should check with your veterinarian and do your own research before following any of these suggestions:

- Owners of susceptible breeds should educate themselves regarding the early signs of bloat and contact their veterinarian as soon as possible if GDV is suspected.
- Owners of susceptible breeds should develop a good working relationship with a local veterinarian in case emergency care is necessary.
- Large dogs should be fed two or three times daily, rather than once a day, and rapid eating should be discouraged.
- Water should be available at all times, but should be limited immediately after feeding. Water weighs 8.2 pounds per gallon, and taking in a large volume of water with food can cause a dog's stomach to swing. Also, do not allow your dog to drink too much water too quickly (as this can cause gulping of air).
- Vigorous exercise, excitement, and stress should be avoided for one hour before and two hours after meals.
- Any diet changes should be made gradually over a period of three to five days.
- Susceptible dogs should be fed individually and, if possible, in a quiet location.
- Some studies suggest that dogs who are susceptible to bloat should not be fed using elevated feeders; other studies have not found this to be true. Experts do recommend, however, that dogs at increased risk be fed at floor level.

- Some studies have shown an association between bloat and food particle size, fat content, moistening of foods containing citric acid, and other diet-related factors. However, at this time, no definitive causal relationships between these factors and bloat have been verified. Discuss any diet change with your veterinarian beforehand.
- Dogs that have survived bloat are at an increased risk for future episodes; therefore, if your dog has survived bloat, discuss preventive surgery or medical management with your veterinarian.
- Dogs with untreated exocrine pancreatic insufficiency (EPI) and/or small intestinal bacterial overgrowth (SIBO) generally produce more gas and thus are at greater risk for bloat. Owners of such dogs should discuss bloat prevention with their veterinarian.
- Do not allow your dog to eat gas-producing foods (especially soybean products, brewer's yeast, and alfalfa).
- Avoid highly stressful situations (experts believe bloat can be brought on by visits to the vet, dog shows, mating, whelping, boarding, the addition of a new dog to the household, a change in the dog's routine, etc.). If you can't avoid these situations, try to minimize the stress as much as possible and watch your dog carefully for signs of distress.
- Feed your dog a high-protein (>30 percent) diet; feeding your dog raw meat is thought to be particularly effective.
- If you feed your dog dry foods, avoid foods that contain citric acid. If you must use a dry food containing citric acid, do not premoisten the food. Select a dry food that includes rendered meat meal with bone product among the first four ingredients.
- Reduce carbohydrates in your dog's diet as much as pos-

sible (carbohydrates are found in many commercial dog biscuits).
- Feed your dog a high-quality diet. Whole, unprocessed foods are especially beneficial.
- Make sure your dog consumes an adequate amount of fiber (for commercial dog food, at least 3 percent crude fiber).
- Add an enzyme product to your dog's food (Prozyme is one such product).
- Include herbs specially mixed for pets that reduce gas in your dog's diet (e.g., N.R. Special Blend).
- Promote an acidic environment in your dog's intestines. Some experts recommend giving your dog one to two tablespoons of aloe vera gel or one tablespoon of apple cider vinegar after each meal.
- Promote "friendly" bacteria in the intestine by including probiotics such as supplemental acidophilus in your dog's diet.
- Be extra cautious on hot days.

For dogs with a high risk of bloat, veterinarians sometimes perform a procedure called a gastropexy, which essentially tacks the right side of the stomach to the right side of the body wall using minimally invasive surgery. A scope is inserted into the dog's belly cavity and an instrument port is created on the front right side of the abdomen. The right side of the stomach is then picked up with a laparoscopic instrument. The instrument port incision is enlarged to one-and-a-half inches and the stomach is then sutured to the right body wall. This procedure can reduce the chances that a dog will suffer from bloat, although it does not prevent it completely. Many breeders prefer not to perform this operation for several different reasons.

K9 MEDIC

Breed	GDV Risk Ratio	Risk Rank
Great Dane	41.4	1
Saint Bernard	21.8	2
Weimaraner	19.3	3
Irish Setter	14.2	4
Gordon Setter	12.3	5
Standard Poodle	8.8	6
Basset Hound	5.9	7
Doberman Pinscher	5.5	8
Old English Sheepdog	4.8	9
German Shorthaired Pointer	4.6	10
Newfoundland	4.4	11
German Shepherd	4.2	12
Airedale Terrier	4.1	13
Alaskan Malamute	4.1	14
Chesapeake Bay Retriever	3.7	15
Boxer	3.7	16
Collie	2.8	17
Labrador Retriever	2	18
English Springer Spaniel	2	19
Samoyed	1.6	20
Dachshund	1.6	21
Golden Retriever	1.2	22
Rottweiler	1.1	23
Mixed-Breed Dog	1.0	24
Miniature Poodle	0.3	25

Source: The University of Purdue

CHAPTER 13
POISONS

Do you know that the most common way dogs are poisoned is by consuming *their owner's* medication? Leaving your medicine out where a dog can reach it could prove to be fatal. There are also many other common household substances that can be fatal to a dog if ingested. You must learn what substances are most likely to poison your dog and take measures to prevent your pet from being exposed to these items. You must also educate yourself regarding what to do if your dog is exposed to a toxin or poison.

Time is of the essence when it comes to poisoning! Have a plan in place regarding whom you will call in the event that your dog is accidentally poisoned. There are several different options that offer different levels of information:
- Your nearest twenty-four-hour emergency veterinary clinic
- ASPCA Poison Control 888-426-4435 (fee required)
- Animal Poison Hotline 888-232-8870 (fee required)
- Pet Poison Hotline 800-213-6680 (fee required)

If you suspect that your dog has been poisoned, you will need to do some investigation before calling one of these services. First, check the dog's vital signs. Next, do your best to discover when the dog took the medication, whether or not he has vomited, and whether the medication is affecting his body. You will also need to know your dog's weight. Have as much of this information as possible on hand before calling for assistance. The treatment options you receive will be much more likely to save your dog depending on how much information you are able to provide.

You probably noticed that most of these services charge a fee. So why can't your veterinarian tell you what you need to know (for free)? Your veterinarian is the perfect place to go for checkups and general illnesses. But seeking information from a specialist offers you a much better chance for a positive outcome in the case of poisoning. The ASPCA has information regarding approximately 1,600,000 case files on hand—information that might just save your pet's life in the event of an emergency.

The following are critical signs of poisoning that require immediate action:
- Blue, white, or very pale gums
- Labored breathing
- Collapse or loss of consciousness

POISONS

- Dizziness, loss of balance, or circling
- Inability to walk
- Extremely bloated abdomen
- Seizures
- Signs of acute, severe pain
- Body temperature over 104°F or under 99°F (normal body temperature for a dog is typically between 100°F and 102.5°F)

Pay special attention if you suspect poison and your dog is vomiting. You should also suspect poison if your dog was behaving normally and then suddenly changed drastically.

There are also several less-critical signs of poisoning. Contact your veterinarian if you notice any of the following signs lasting for more than one to two days:

- Poor appetite
- Lethargy
- Vomiting
- Diarrhea
- Lameness
- Weakness
- Excessive salivation
- Excessive thirst (indicated by increased water intake)
- Frequent and/or inappropriate urination
- Constipation
- Excessive scratching or dull, dry, or flaky coat
- Wheezing or frequent panting
- Nasal discharge or congestion
- Displays of mild to moderate pain

If your dog has consumed a caustic substance, it is important to avoid inducing vomiting. Caustic substances burn the internal tissues. If it burns going down, it will burn coming back up, too. Caustic chemicals and substances include but are not limited to:
- Battery acid
- Carbolic acid
- Motor oil
- Drain cleaner
- Fertilizer
- Glue
- Household cleaners
- Kerosene
- Laundry detergent
- Turpentine
- Plaster
- Sidewalk salt
- Putty
- Pine-scented cleaners
- Paintbrush cleaner
- Nail polish
- Nail polish remover
- Paint thinner

Poisonous Substances
Although a list of substances that can be poisonous to dogs could take up a whole book by itself, I have included what I consider my top ten here.

Prescription human medications. Dogs are notorious for ingesting anything that is dropped, including pills. Always be sure to take your own medications in a safe place away from your pet. Your

POISONS

dog is much smaller than you are, and ingesting your medication could therefore be fatal for him.

Insecticides and chemicals. Poisoning by insecticide was the subject of 11 percent of calls to the ASPCA poison control hotline in 2011. These include products used on lawns, in the house, and on your pet. Take the time to read all warnings and instructions before you use any insecticide, and never use a product labeled for dogs on cats.

Over-the-counter human medications. Over-the-counter medications such as ibuprofen can kill your pet. Never give any medication to your pet without first consulting with your veterinarian.

People food. Chocolate is the most common "people food" regarding which dog owners call poison help numbers. Too much chocolate can cause vomiting, diarrhea, elevated heart rate, and seizures. Chocolate and cocoa contain a chemical called theobromide that can adversely affect the heart, lungs, kidney, and central nervous system. Pure baking chocolate is the most toxic, while milk chocolate requires a higher quantity to cause harm. A twenty-pound dog can be poisoned after consuming about two ounces of baking chocolate, but it would take nearly twenty ounces of milk chocolate to cause harm. Ingestion of cacao bean mulch can also be toxic. Signs of theobromide poisoning include excitement, tremors, seizures, vomiting, diarrhea, abnormal heart rate/rhythm, drunken gait, hyperthermia, and coma. Your vet may induce vomiting or perform gastric lavage. Treatment includes administration of activated charcoal and aggressive supportive care with fluid therapy and medications.

Caffeine affects dogs in much the same way as the toxic chemical in chocolate. It can damage the heart, lungs, kidneys, and central nervous system. Dogs can suffer from caffeine poisoning after ingesting caffeine pills, coffee beans or coffee, large amounts of tea, and chocolate, among other things. Symptoms typically begin with restlessness, hyperactivity, and vomiting. These can be followed by panting, weakness, drunken gait, increased heart rate, muscle tremors, and convulsions. Your vet may induce vomiting or perform gastric lavage. Treatment includes administration of activated charcoal and supportive care with fluid therapy and medications.

The second most common problem food for dogs is xylitol. Xylitol is a sugar-free sweetener most often found in chewing gum and candy. In dogs, it stimulates the pancreas to secrete insulin, resulting in hypoglycemia (low blood sugar). Xylitol ingestion can cause severe liver damage. As few as two pieces of gum can cause hypoglycemia (low blood sugar) in a twenty-pound dog. A pack of gum can cause liver damage. Signs of toxicity can occur within thirty to sixty minutes and include weakness, drunken gait, collapse, and seizures. Your vet may induce vomiting or perform gastric lavage. The affected dog will likely need to be treated intravenously with dextrose (sugar) and monitored closely for one to two days. Many dogs improve with supportive care if treated early enough, though the liver damage caused by Xylitol can be permanent.

Grapes and raisins can cause irreversible damage to a dog's kidneys, possibly resulting in death. Ingesting as few as four to five grapes or raisins can be poisonous to a twenty-pound dog, though the exact toxic dose has not been determined. Signs of poisoning due to grapes and raisins include vomiting, loss of appetite, diarrhea, abdominal pain, decreased urine production (possibly leading to lack of urine production), weakness, and abnormal gait. Onset of these signs typically occurs within twenty-four hours (though they can start just a few hours after consumption). To treat your pet, your vet may start by inducing vomiting, or the stomach might be pumped. Treatment generally involves aggressive supportive care, particularly fluid therapy and medications.

POISONS

Onions can cause a form of hemolytic anemia called Heinz body anemia, a condition that causes the destruction of red blood cells. Kidney damage may follow. Dogs can also be poisoned by similar foods, including garlic and chives. It is not clear what quantity of onions is poisonous, but the effects can be cumulative. Poisoning can result from consuming raw, cooked, and dehydrated forms of this vegetable. Avoid feeding your dog table scraps or any foods cooked with onions (including some baby foods). Check your ingredients! The symptoms of onion poisoning include pale gums, rapid heart rate, weakness, lethargy, vomiting, diarrhea, and bloody urine. Treatment includes blood transfusions and/or oxygen administration followed by specific fluid therapy.

Macadamia nuts, while generally not considered fatal, can make your dog very ill. The actual toxin is not known, nor is the mechanism of toxicity. Ingestion of just a handful of nuts can cause adverse effects in any dog. Signs include vomiting, weakness, depression, drunken gait, joint/muscle pain, and joint swelling. Onset of symptoms typically occurs within six to twenty-four hours.

Household products. Dogs have been known to eat anything from fire logs to paint. Some household items may only cause stomach upset, while others can be deadly.

Veterinary medications. Chewable medications make it easy to give your dog a pill. However, making medications taste good can also mean that the pet, if given access, will ingest all the pills in the bottle. Always make sure to keep pet medications out of reach.

Rodenticides. When putting out bait to kill mice and rats, never underestimate the resourcefulness of your pet. Most bait is grain-based, making it attractive to dogs. Depending on the type of rodenticide, ingestion can cause internal bleeding, kidney failure, or seizures.

Plants. Many calls to poison hotlines are about animals eating plants. While this is one category in which cats beat out dogs in the number of exposures, many types of plants and flowers can be poisonous to your dog. Effects range from mild to severe depending on the type of plant and the quantity consumed. Some plants will only cause slight stomach upset, while others can cause seizures, coma, or even death. Water hemlock is the most violently toxic plant that grows in North America. Only a small amount of the toxic substance in the plant is needed to produce poisoning in livestock or in humans. The toxin cicutoxin, acting directly on the central nervous system, is a violent convulsant. Clinical signs of poisoning occur when a threshold dose is reached after which grand mal seizures and death occur. Just one root from this plant can kill a cow. Learn about the plants in your yard and neighborhood that are dangerous and be sure your dog does not have access to them. Remove any toxic plants on your own property. Houseplants are a bit easier to control: simply do not keep toxic plants inside your home, and you have removed the risk. If you are planning to get new plants or flowers, research them ahead of time to learn if they are toxic to your pet. Take the time to look into common toxic plants and flowers.

Lawn and garden products. Fertilizers can be made of dried blood, poultry manure, and bone meal, all substances that can be very attractive to pets. It is not surprising that poison hotlines get many calls concerning lawn and garden items.

Automotive products. With more people keeping their animals inside (especially cats), the number of animals exposed to automotive products (antifreeze, brake fluid, etc.) has dropped. This is great news, since many of these products can be life threatening to pets if ingested.

CHAPTER 14
HEAT STROKE AND FROSTBITE

Heat stroke can develop into a potentially deadly situation in dogs in just a few minutes. This usually happens when a dog is in a closed space, such as a car, where the temperature steadily climbs. In some instances, heat stroke can take hours to develop into a deadly situation.

Heat stroke is a condition that occurs when the dog's body absorbs more heat than it can release. When this happens, the temperature inside the dog's body begins to climb. Once the temperature reaches a certain point, the dog's body is unable to regulate normal functions, and the result is heat stroke. Once heat stroke occurs, damage to the dog's muscles, organs, and metabolic processes can occur.

Heat stroke in dogs is a potentially life-threatening condition that requires immediate medical treatment. It can often be fatal.

Dogs can be in danger of heat stroke if they are confined in a hot space, or if they have worked or played too much without taking cooling down periods. Sadly, this condition is quite common, especially in dogs that live in hot and/or humid climates. Older or overweight dogs are more susceptible to injury and death due to heat stroke.

Never leave your pet in a parked car! Even with the windows open slightly, your pet can quickly suffer heat stroke and even die. Temperatures can exceed 120°F in a parked car! In this environment, your dog's internal temperature can get as hot as 110°F.

Dogs pant to help control their internal temperature, but they do not sweat (except for a very small amount in the pads of the feet, which is not nearly enough to counteract the effects of overheating). In the case of heat stroke, panting is not enough to cool the body.

Heat stroke becomes a very serious condition if the dog's body temperature rises above 104°F. The dog may exhibit the following signs:

- Collapse
- Bloody diarrhea or bloody vomit
- Depression
- Seizures
- Coma
- Excessive panting or difficulty breathing
- Increased heart rate
- Increased respiratory rate
- Redder than normal mucous membrane color
- Excess salivation

If your dog is hotter than 104°F, you will need to spray or soak him with cool water. If using an outdoor hose, run the water for a minute or so before spraying your pet to make sure any hot water in the

HEAT STROKE AND FROSTBITE

hose is gone. Spray your dog for a minute or two, and then retake his temperature. Further treatment includes placing water-soaked towels on the dog's head, neck, feet, chest, and abdomen. You should also turn on a fan and point it in your dog's direction.

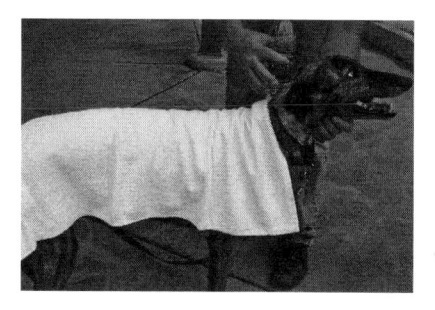

Place a cool, wet towel over the dog's back.

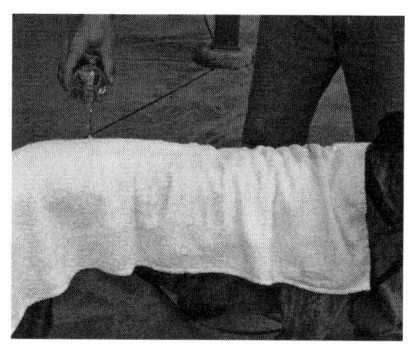

Use water to cool the dog's entire body.

The goal is to decrease your dog's body temperature to 103°F in the first ten to fifteen minutes after heat stroke occurs. Once 103°F is reached, you must stop the cooling process. This is because the dog's body temperature can become dangerously low if you continue to cool the dog.

Even if you successfully cool your pet down to 103°F, you must take him to a veterinarian as soon as possible. This is because many of the consequences of hyperthermia don't show up for hours or even days.

Dogs can also suffer from frostbite. Frostbite is a condition that occurs as a result of exposure to freezing or sub-freezing temperatures. In dogs, it most commonly affects the tips of the ears, the tail, and the feet (especially the toes).

The blood flowing through your dog's blood vessels supplies not only oxygen and nutrients to tissues, but also heat. If a portion of the body, such as an ear, becomes very cold, the blood vessels in that area become smaller to help the body conserve heat. The tissues in that ear will then have less blood supply, which means they can eventually become as cold as the surrounding temperatures. If the tissue actually freezes, it will die. The risk is increased in windy conditions or if the animal is wet.

Initially, frostbitten tissue may appear pale or gray in color. The area will be cold to the touch and may feel hard. As the area thaws, it may become red. As the tissue warms, frostbite becomes very painful.

In severe frostbite, the tissue will start to appear black in color within several days and will begin to slough off over the course of several weeks. The tissue at this point will generally not be painful.

If you can, warm the affected area rapidly with warm (*never hot*) water. The recommended water temperature is 90°F to 104°F. Use warm compresses or soak the affected area in a bowl of warm water. Do *not* use direct dry heat, such as a heating pad or hair dryer. Do not use chemical heat packs, as they are just too hot. After you

HEAT STROKE AND FROSTBITE

have warmed the area, dry it gently and thoroughly. Do not rub or massage the affected area. Contact your veterinarian or emergency clinic and have your pet examined immediately. In severe cases in which a large amount of tissue has died, it may be necessary to amputate the affected area.

CHAPTER 15
ADMINISTERING MEDICATIONS

Because giving medications is not something you do every day, it can be a little tricky. The following guidelines can help make administering medications easier for you and safer for your dog.

As a general rule, it's important to remember never to give medications by mouth to an animal who is lying down, unconscious, vomiting, having trouble breathing, or having a seizure.

ADMINISTERING MEDICATIONS

Administering Eye Medications

Rest the hand that you will use to administer the medication on the bone above your dog's upper eyelid. This will help to prevent poking the medication tube into the eye. Tilt the dog's head backward slightly, with the palm of your other hand under the chin, supporting the head. With this same hand, pull down the lower eyelid with your thumb. Place the drops or ointment directly into the eye from far enough away to ensure that the tip of the dispenser does not touch the eye.

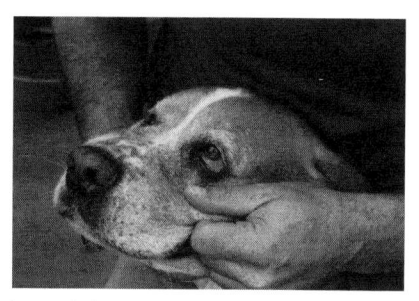

Pull the eyelid down so you can access the lower lid.

If you are flushing the eye, make sure the healthy eye is on top. You do not want to flush bad stuff into a healthy eye.

Administering Ear Medications

Stand on the same side of the animal as the ear you will be treating. If the dog is floppy-eared, lift the floppy portion so you can clearly see into the ear. Place the drops or ointment in the middle of the ear opening. Rub or massage the base of the ear to allow the medication to drop down into the deeper portion of the ear.

Never put your finger further into a dog's ear than you can see.

Liquid Medications

Liquid medications are generally easier to administer than other medications. The hardest part is doing the conversion from teaspoons to cubic centimeters (cc) or milliliters (ml). Here are some common conversions:

- one milliliter = one cc. These measurements are actually the same amount, but you might see one or the other on a syringe
- Approximately five cc = one teaspoon
- fifteen cc = one tablespoon

To administer liquid medications, place the end of the eyedropper or syringe on one side of your dog's mouth, in the corner of the lips, just behind the pointy canine teeth. Gently position the dropper above the lower teeth; then place it in the pouch between the gums and the lower teeth. Slowly administer the medication, giving it no faster than the animal can swallow.

Pills and Capsules

With one hand, hold your pet's upper jaw toward the ceiling by taking hold of the snout and gently pointing it upward. This will cause the lower jaw to drop slightly. With the other hand, gently pull down on the very front-most part of the lower jaw. Place the tablet in the center of the back of the tongue as far back in the mouth as you can safely reach. Once you have given the pill, hold the dog's mouth closed until your pet licks her nose or swallows.

Pills can also be hidden in food, but you must ensure that your pet does not simply eat the food and spit out the pill. Peanut butter works well for this.

ADMINISTERING MEDICATIONS

There are also commercial pill "guns" available. These plastic tubes hold the pill and allow you to place it in the back of the dog's throat without putting your hands in the animal's mouth. Some people also suggest having your dog sit with his back in a corner while giving a pill to discourage an escape.

Topical Ointments and Creams
Apply the medication in a thin layer. The big challenge will be keeping your dog from licking the ointment. It works better on the skin, not in the stomach! You might want to place an Elizabethan collar on your dog to prevent her from licking the medication. You might also consider using one of your old T-shirts or boxer shorts to cover the affected area.

Elizabethan Collars (E-Collars)
These collars are obviously designed for function, not fashion! They're extremely helpful for keeping your dog from aggravating a wound, biting sutures, or licking off ointments and creams. This is a good tool to have, but your dog will need time to get used to it. He may bang into walls and furniture due to lack of peripheral vision. This is only temporary. Elizabethan collars can be purchased from any pet supply store or from your veterinarian.

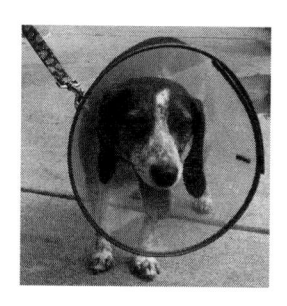

CHAPTER 16
OTHER INJURIES AND ILLNESSES

In this chapter, I will cover many other dog illnesses and injuries that you may need to know how to handle in the event of an emergency.

Vomiting
Vomiting can be frightening to witness. Nevertheless, while not normal, most of the time it is a temporary condition and your dog will be fine. However, there are some conditions under which vomiting can be of special concern.

OTHER INJURIES AND ILLNESSES

If vomiting continues after you withhold food for a day (as long as the dog is an otherwise healthy adult), it could signal a more serious problem; also, your dog will be at risk for dehydration. If your dog is dry heaving without producing any vomit, it could signal bloat. If your dog vomits intermittently within the time span of a month or several months and also has diarrhea and weight loss, it could signal inflammatory bowel disease.

The other most common causes of vomiting are:
- Bacterial, viral, or parasitic infection
- Change in diet
- Eating something that upsets the stomach
- Eating something that cannot pass through the gastrointestinal tract and becomes stuck
- Eating toxic materials, including many types of plants
- Glandular disease
- Linear foreign bodies (i.e., string, rope, or panty hose that become trapped while traveling through the stomach and intestines, bunching the intestines and sawing through the intestinal walls)
- Motion sickness
- Organ inflammation, infection, or failure, which can be caused by kidney disease or pancreatitis
- Many other illnesses and issues

If your dog is vomiting but otherwise acting normally, a conservative approach is best. If your dog is relatively young and otherwise healthy and normal, withhold food and water for eight to twelve hours. Elderly dogs (over ten years old), very young dogs (under one year), or otherwise ill animals should not go without food or water; they should be examined by a veterinarian.

If vomiting ceases when food and water are withheld, offer the animal a small quantity of ice chips and repeat every two to three hours as long as vomiting does not recur.

If no vomiting occurs for six hours after giving ice chips, add a small amount of water (a quarter of a cup for a small dog, a third of a cup for a medium-sized dog, and half a cup for a large or very large dog) or pediatric electrolyte oral solution in addition to the water. Repeat every two to three hours as long as vomiting does not recur.

If your dog is still not vomiting after eight to twelve hours, add some bland or high-fiber food. Give two teaspoons at a time for small dogs, one tablespoon at a time for medium-sized dogs, and two tablespoons at a time for large and very large dogs. Repeat every few hours as long as no vomiting occurs.

Use the following size ranges for food and water rationing after vomiting:

- Small dog: twenty pounds or less
- Medium-sized dog: twenty-one to forty-nine pounds
- Large dog: sixty-one to one hundred pounds
- Giant dog: one hundred pounds or more

If no vomiting occurs during the next forty-eight to seventy-two hours, increase the amount of food and decrease the frequency. During the next three to five days, gradually mix the animal's regular diet with the bland diet, slowly returning to a normal dietary regimen.

If vomiting occurs despite withholding food and water, or if vomiting occurs when you reintroduce water and/or food, you must take the animal to a veterinarian to rule out any serious and possibly life-threatening conditions, and also to treat the animal for possible dehydration and nausea.

OTHER INJURIES AND ILLNESSES

If other signs of illness accompany the vomiting, such as fever or lethargy, do not withhold food and water. Take the animal directly to a veterinarian.

It is important to be aware that rapid dehydration can occur if the animal is not eating or drinking and is losing body fluids as a result of vomiting and/or diarrhea. Dehydration can lead to shock and death. Giving ice cubes or ice chips instead of water can prevent dehydration and keep a dog from drinking too much water too soon.

Jellyfish Stings

Jellyfish stings are definitely not deadly, but they can be quite painful. Signs and symptoms of a jellyfish sting include pain, the presence of the stinger, and swelling.

You can usually treat jellyfish stings with your first-aid kit. Pour rubbing alcohol on any tentacles left in the skin. This will help stabilize the toxins. Use sticky tape to remove any jellyfish tentacles from the dog's fur. Make a paste of baking soda and water and apply it to the affected area. This will soothe the irritation. Administer diphenhydramine (Benadryl'). The dose is one to two milligrams per pound of your dog's weight. Never give a dog more than fifty milligrams of diphenhydramine.

Toads

The vast majority of toads are not poisonous. But there are some poisonous toads, including the Colorado River toad (found mainly in the southwest United States) and the giant brown toad or marine toad (found in Florida, south Texas, and Hawaii). These toads can kill a dog within thirty minutes. The poisons on a toad's skin can cause severe discomfort and even paralysis or death.

If you notice the remains of a toad in your dog's mouth or if you see your dog licking a toad or its remains, call your veterinarian. While most contact with a toad is not fatal, the toad's skin has a profound effect that can cause your dog to salivate a white froth and lick his mouth for about six hours. This time will be reduced if you are able to wash the dog's mouth out soon after exposure.

Some other common signs and symptoms of exposure to toad toxin include:
- Collapse
- Diarrhea
- Excess salivation
- Fever
- Pawing at the mouth
- Seizures
- Vomiting
- Weakness

If you suspect your dog has been exposed to toad toxin, flush out the dog's mouth with water. Call your veterinarian immediately. If it's determined that he has been poisoned, it's likely your dog will need to stay overnight for treatment.

Snakebites
This book covers only snakes found in the United States. The main class of snakes that you need to be concerned about is pit vipers. This category includes rattlesnakes, copperheads, and cottonmouths.

If your dog is bitten by a snake, you will need to try to identify the kind of snake involved. However, never put yourself in harm's way to identify a snake! The good news is that you may be able to identify it from a safe distance.

OTHER INJURIES AND ILLNESSES

Pit vipers have a depression between their nose and eyes. They have retractable fangs and their heads are triangular. Nonpoisonous snakes have a rounded head and the eyes are filled in (there is no pupil in the eye). Rattlesnakes can be up to eight feet in length and their tails contain a rattle. Copperheads are about four feet long and have no rattles. The top of the head is a rich, coppery orange color. Cottonmouths, also known as water moccasins, can grow to four feet long. The body is dark and the inside of the mouth is snowy white. Coral snakes have nonretractable fangs in the rear of the mouth. They can be up to three feet long. Their coloration is red, yellow, and black in alternating bands.

Another way to determine if a snake is poisonous is to look at the last foot or so of the snake's tail. This area is called the anal plate. If there is a "seam" (or what looks like a line running lengthwise down the snake), chances are it is nonpoisonous.

If you are forced to kill a snake to protect yourself or your pet, be aware that the fangs on a decapitated snake's head may still be venomous for up to one and a half hours after the snake's death.

If your dog is bitten by a snake, she needs to be seen by a vet as soon as possible. Snakebite deaths are much more common in dogs than in humans (for whom they are actually quite rare) because dogs are so much smaller than people.

The signs and symptoms of snakebite include:
- A bleeding puncture wound
- Blood does not clot
- Breathing stops
- Bruising or sloughing of the skin over the bitten area
- Fang marks may or may not be visible, due to dog hair
- Neurological symptoms such as twitching and drooling
- Pallor or pale skin around the area of the bite
- Reddening

- Signs of shock
- Swelling around the area of the bite

If you suspect your dog has been bitten by a snake, remove the dog from the area. If you are able, carry the animal. This will keep the heart rate down and reduce the spread of the venom. Attempt to keep the animal calm and still. Wash the wound with water and mild soap. Do *not* cut open the wound or attempt to suck out the venom. Do *not* place ice on the area or use a tourniquet. Immediately transport your dog to a veterinary hospital.

Dogs can also be bitten by nonpoisonous snakes. While these bites are not generally dangerous, they can cause local tissue trauma. They may also cause an allergic reaction. Treat nonpoisonous snakebites as you would any puncture wound, and watch for allergic reactions.

Scorpions
Being stung by a scorpion is an emergency, especially a sting from the more rare bark scorpion. Know the scorpions in your area and get your dog to a veterinarian immediately if you suspect she has been stung by a scorpion. Signs and symptoms of a scorpion sting include:
- Accidental urination and defecation
- Breathing problems
- Collapse and potential death
- Dilated pupils
- Drooling
- Pain
- Paralysis
- Swelling
- Tearing from the eyes

OTHER INJURIES AND ILLNESSES

There is not much you can do if your dog is stung by a scorpion. Take your dog to a veterinarian immediately for treatment.

Smoke Inhalation

Smoke inhalation is a life-threatening emergency. In fact, smoke can be more deadly than burns. Often dogs who are involved in a house fire inhale a great deal of smoke, as well as suffering airway burns and airway swelling, which can all be life threating. The worst-case scenario is that the animal will simply stop breathing.

Many consequences of smoke inhalation may not be apparent for days. If your dog is exposed to fire or smoke, watch her breathing and take her to the veterinarian immediately. Signs and symptoms of smoke inhalation include:

- Abnormally fast breathing
- Cherry-red gums (caused by carbon monoxide poisoning)
- Coughing
- Discharge from the mouth, nose, or eyes
- Labored breathing
- No breathing
- Singed hair and/or a smoky odor to the coat

If you suspect your dog is suffering from smoke inhalation, immediately remove him from the smoke and get him into fresh air. Check his airway, breathing, and circulation. Take your dog to a veterinary hospital immediately.

Car Accidents

Even the best-trained dogs can be hit or struck by a moving vehicle. The worst-case scenario would be you actually backing over your own dog. While this may be horrible to think about, it happens all too

K9 MEDIC

often. While we cannot prevent all accidents, there are some prevention tips you can follow to protect your dog from being injured by a car:

- *Always* be sure to look around and under your car before backing up.
- *Never* transport your dog in the back of an open pickup truck.
- It is best to keep your dog as an indoor pet and make sure they are leashed when outdoors.
- Invest in a seat belt harness. It would be unthinkable to let our children ride in a vehicle with no safety restraint system. We must take the same approach for our dogs. It is important to note there are many different restraint systems for dogs, however only ONE passed the Federal Motor Vehicle for Safety Standards at time of this publication. You can visit online the Center for Pet Safety for more information.

If your dog is hit by a car, try to pinpoint the area on his body that was hit and whether your dog was simply hit or was driven over or thrown by the collision. Often, even in very serious cases, a dog will get up and attempt to walk away after being hit by a car. This does not necessarily mean that he is not severely injured; it is the dog's instinctive response to try to escape danger.

Remember your safety. Approach the scene cautiously. Alert oncoming traffic. Paramedics always say that slow or stopped traffic is the best traffic. Remember that you are your dog's medic, and you will not be able to help him if you are also injured.

If the dog cannot move, he may have a broken back or severe internal injuries, and may also be in shock. If your dog cannot move or appears to have a spinal injury, place her on a flat board for transport. (See more information regarding this technique in chapter 11.) If you cannot find a board, use a blanket or a shirt. Slide your dog onto the

OTHER INJURIES AND ILLNESSES

fabric and have one or two people hold it as stiffly as possible on each side.

Check to see if the dog's airway is open. Is he breathing? Is the breathing labored? Is there a heartbeat or a pulse? If not, unfortunately the animal's chances for a good outcome are quite slim. Injuries caused by a car are often just too devastating for a dog to survive.

If your dog is alert and standing, observe whether he is limping or favoring one side. Look for blood, open wounds, bruising, or limbs hanging in an abnormal position. Control all bleeding and check for shock.

There are many internal injuries that may not show up for twelve to seventy-two hours after a traumatic incident. These can include slow leakage of blood from internal organs, rupture of the urinary bladder or other internal organs, and air or blood leaking into the chest cavity. Because the dog's body is initially attempting to compensate for the trauma, early shock may be difficult to identify. Have your dog checked by a veterinarian after any accident involving a car, even if she seems uninjured.

Encounters with Wild Animals

Dogs who are allowed to roam freely often come across wildlife such as skunks and porcupines. This can lead to very unpleasant experiences. To avoid this problem, keep your dog on a leash.

Porcupines are vegetarian rodents known for their unique coat, consisting of about thirty thousand quills. Contrary to popular belief, porcupines do not shoot or eject their quills. When they feel threatened, tiny muscles in the skin make the quills "stand up" in defense. A swipe of the tail will leave a bunch of needlelike quills in whatever the tail happens to touch.

If your dog has only a few quills embedded in her skin and you are certain there are none in the mouth or throat, you can try to remove them with a pair of pliers. Be aware that this will be a painful experience for your dog, so it is best to muzzle her before attempting to remove the quills and to have someone available to help you restrain the animal. It may help to cover your dog's eyes so she doesn't see the pliers approaching. Speak to her in soft, soothing tones. Firmly grab the quill with the pliers close to the skin. Be prepared for your dog to jerk backward, separating herself from the quill.

Even when there are only a few quills, a trip to the vet for assistance and pain medicine might be a better choice for the comfort of the dog. If there are numerous or deeply embedded quills, or if quills are affecting your dog's eyes, mouth, or throat, take her to your veterinarian immediately.

The most notorious feature of skunks is the spray produced by their anal scent glands, which they can use as a defensive weapon. Skunks have two glands, one on each side of the anus. These glands produce a mixture of sulfur-containing chemicals such as methyl and butyl thiols, traditionally called mercaptans, which have a highly offensive smell. Muscles located next to the scent glands allow them to spray with a high degree of accuracy for as far as ten feet (three meters). The odor of this fluid is strong enough to ward off bears and other potential attackers and can be difficult to remove from clothing. It is so powerful that the human nose can detect it up to a mile downwind. The smell aside, skunk spray can also cause skin and eye irritation and even temporary blindness.

OTHER INJURIES AND ILLNESSES

Illinois chemist Paul Krebaum has developed an effective formula for neutralizing skunk spray:
- one quart of 3 percent hydrogen peroxide
- 1/4 cup of baking soda
- one teaspoon of liquid soap

Apply this mixture to sprayed areas, and then wash off with tap water. The solution must be mixed as needed; it can't be stored in a bottle or other container.

Drowning

Dogs are typically good swimmers. But you still must always keep an eye on your dog when near any body of water. There are several situations in which a dog might be at risk of drowning, including.
- Animal abuse
- Boating accidents
- Falling through thin ice or falling into water
- Being unable to exit a swimming pool
- Small dog left unattended during a bath in the bathtub
- Swimming too far out and becoming fatigued or experiencing muscle cramps

After you remove the dog from the water, for an unconscious small dog, lift the dog up by the hind legs to allow water to come out of his nose or mouth. Then start CPR. For an unconscious dog that is too large to be lifted in this way, lift the hind legs (with the front end on the ground) so gravity can expel the water. Then start CPR.

If you are able to revive your dog, you should still take him to the veterinarian when he is stabilized. This is necessary due to the possibility of fluid buildup in the lungs, as well as the effects of hypothermia.

Electric Shock

Electric shock or electrocution injuries generally occur when dogs bite electrical cords. This is typically more common with puppies.

In cases of severe electrocution, electrical current disrupts the natural conduction of the heart. The dog will need CPR in order to survive. More minor electrocution can cause an electrical burn to the mouth. A dog with a mouth injury due to electrocution may exhibit coughing, drooling, difficulty breathing, or have a foul odor from the mouth. Also look for ulcers inside the mouth affecting the tongue, roof, and the cheek and gums. Loss of appetite may be another sign of this type of injury.

Remember your own safety when electrocution is a risk. Be sure to turn off the power to and unplug the cord of the appliance that has caused the injury. *Do not* attempt to free your dog from the cord if the power is on and the cord is still plugged in. If you cannot turn off the power at the source, turn off the power to the house. Then check the dog's airway, breathing, and circulation and perform CPR if necessary.

Again, while no one can prevent all accidents, there are some preventive tips that can help keep your dog safe from electrocution:

- Use plastic sleeves or cord covers to prevent access to electric cords.
- Place cords in inaccessible locations whenever possible.
- Unplug all electrical cords when not in use.
- Provide appropriate toys for chewing puppies.
- If you see your pet showing interest in a cord, rub the cord with a hot pepper sauce or other deterrents (such as the Bitter Apple® product available at pet supply stores).

OTHER INJURIES AND ILLNESSES

Fishhook Injuries

The most likely places for dogs to be injured by fishhooks are around the face and muzzle, inside the mouth, and on the paws. It is also possible for a dog to swallow a fishhook whole.

If you can't get your dog to a veterinarian immediately, push the hook through the exit wound until the barb is visible. Cut the barb off with a wire cutter. With the barb removed, pull the hook out backward, the way it went in.

If the hook is embedded inside the mouth, or if a hook (with or without the line attached) is swallowed, immediately transport your dog to a veterinary hospital. Do not attempt to pull out the hook!

Nosebleeds

Dogs usually get nosebleeds only as a result of injury or blunt trauma. However, a small amount of blood from one nostril may be an early sign of a tumor or bleeding disorder. In either case, your dog should see a veterinarian as soon as possible.

Eye Injuries

A dog's eyes can be dislocated from their sockets by trauma (i.e., being hit by a car, a bite wound, etc.) or, rarely, due to overly aggressive holding of the neck or pulling of the collar, particularly in dogs with small snouts and big eyes, such as Pekingese. This type of injury can be very upsetting to witness. Do your best to stay calm. Do not allow the dog to paw or scratch at the eye. Apply sterile eyewash to keep the eye from drying out while transporting your dog to a veterinary hospital. Your veterinarian will decide whether it is feasible to try to put the eye back in or whether it makes more sense to remove it. Even if the eye is put back, vision usually will not be restored.

Eyes can also be injured by foreign objects. A dog can suffer minor eye irritation due to flying debris or from brushing up against a plant. These issues can be handled at home. Gently wash the eye with large amounts of either tap water or sterile saline eyewash. Sterile saline eyewash is preferable; it is available at any pharmacy and should be a part of your first-aid kit. Inspect the eye with a strong light source to ensure the foreign object is completely gone.

Even if you are able to flush out the foreign object, you should contact your veterinarian. Foreign objects can cause a corneal ulcer or lead to infections.

Toenail Injuries
If you have ever cared for a dog with a bloody nail, you know it can be quite messy. The dewclaws (the thumb toes higher on the foot) are very susceptible to tearing. This is because they don't reach the ground and are not subject to normal wear, so they are far more tender than the other pads. Use care when clipping your dog's nails, and always use nail clippers that are specifically designed for dogs.

If the nail is bleeding, apply styptic powder to the area. This should be a part of your pet first-aid kit. You can also try applying direct pressure to the nail with a piece of gauze or clean cloth for five minutes. If you do not have these items available, you can take a bar of soap and push it into the bleeding nail, or apply flour or cornstarch to the area with firm pressure for five minutes. If none of these options stop the bleeding, wrap the paw and transport your dog to a veterinary hospital.

CHAPTER 17
DISASTER PLANNING

When disaster strikes, the same rules that apply to people apply to pets: Preparation makes all the difference, and if it's not safe for you, it's not safe for them.

Here is a checklist of the steps you should take to prepare for a disaster. If you do not plan prior to a disaster it's called reactionary chaos. The sad part is that many pets my not make it through the event or may never be reunited with their owner. Here is what to do.

1. **Start getting ready now**

    Make sure that your dog is wearing a collar and has identification. Make sure that it is up to date and visible at all times. You'll increase your chances of being reunited with a lost pet by having them microchipped.

    Put your cell phone number on your pet's tag.

2. **Put together your disaster kit**

    Stock up on all non-perishables ahead of time, and have everything ready to go at a moment's notice. Keep everything accessible and stored in sturdy containers that can be carried easily. Any dry pet food should be stored in airtight containers and refreshed every six months. If you live in an area prone to flooding or hurricanes, make a kit to keep in your car in case you have to evacuate quickly. If you live in an area where tornadoes occur, store supplies in a tornado-proof room or cellar.

Here are some common items found in a basic disaster kit:

- Food and water for at least five days for each pet,
- bowls and a manual can opener if you are packing canned pet food.
- People need at least one gallon of water per person per day. While your pet may not need that much, keep an extra gallon on hand if your pet has been exposed to chemicals or flood waters and needs to be rinsed.
- Medications and medical records stored in a waterproof container and a first-aid kit. A Copy of *K9 Medic* is also handy.
- Garbage bags to collect all pets' waste.
- Sturdy leashes, harnesses, and carriers to transport pets safely and to ensure that your pets can't escape. Carriers should be large enough to allow your pet to stand comfortably, turn around, and lie down. (Your pet may have to stay in the carrier for hours at a time.) Be sure to have a secure cage with no loose objects inside it to accommodate smaller pets—who may also need blankets or towels for bedding and warmth as well as special items, depending on their species.
- Current photos of you with your pets and descriptions of your pets to help others identify them in case you and your pets become separated. This will also help to prove that they are yours once you're reunited.
- Pet beds and toys, if you can easily take them, this will reduce stress.
- Written information about your pets' feeding schedules, medical conditions, and behavior issues along with the name and number of your veterinarian in case you have to board your pets or place them in foster care.

DISASTER PLANNING

3. **Find a safe place to stay ahead of time**

    Some communities have groups that have solely focused on providing emergency sheltering for pets, and other communities simply don't have the resources. That's why you should never assume that you will be allowed to bring your pet to an emergency shelter.

    Before disaster hits call your local office of emergency management to see if you will be allowed to evacuate with your pets and that there will be shelters that take people and their pets in your area. And just to be safe, track down a pet-friendly safe place for your family and pets.

    Contact hotels and motels outside your immediate area to find out if they accept pets. Ask about any restrictions on number, size, and species. Inquire if the "no pet" policies would be waived in an emergency. Keep a list of animal-friendly places handy, and call ahead for a reservation as soon as you think you might have to leave your home.

    Make arrangements with friends or relatives. Ask people outside the immediate area if they would be able to shelter you and your pets—or just your pets—if necessary. If you have more than one pet, you may need to arrange to house them at separate locations.

    Consider a kennel or veterinarian's office. Make a list of boarding facilities and veterinary offices that might be able to shelter animals in disaster emergencies (include their 24-hour telephone numbers).

    As a last resort, ask your local animal shelter. Some shelters may be able to provide foster care or shelter for pets in an emergency. But shelters have limited resources and are likely to be stretched to their limits during an emergency.

    Plan for your pet in case you're not home as disaster or evacuation order may come when you're out of the house. Make arrangements well in advance for a trusted neighbor or nearby friend or family member to take your pets and meet you at a specified location. Be sure the person is comfortable with your pets and your pets are familiar with him or her. Give your emergency caretaker a key to your home and show her or him where your pets are likely to be (or hide) and where your disaster supplies are kept.

4. **If you evacuate, take your pet**

    Rule number one: If it isn't safe for you, it isn't safe for your pets. Even if you think you will only be gone for a few hours, take your pets. You have no way of knowing how long you'll be kept out of the area, and you may not be able, or allowed to, go back for your pets.

    Pets left behind in a disaster can easily be injured, lost, or killed. Those left inside your home can escape through storm-damaged areas, such as broken windows. And pets turned loose to fend for themselves are likely to become victims of exposure, starvation, predators, contaminated food or water, or accidents. Leaving dogs tied or chained outside in a disaster is a sure disaster in itself.

    Rule number two: Evacuate early. Don't wait for a mandatory evacuation order. Some people who have waited to be evacuated by emergency officials have been told to leave their pets behind. The smell of smoke, high winds, or lightning may make your pet more fearful and difficult to load into a crate or carrier. Evacuating before conditions become severe will keep everyone safer and make the process less stressful.

DISASTER PLANNING

5. **If you stay home, do it safely**

    If your family and pets must wait out a storm or other disaster at home, identify a safe area of your home where you can all stay together. Make that safe area animal friendly:

    - Move dangerous items such as tools or toxic products that have been stored.
    - Be sure to close your windows and doors, stay inside, and follow the instructions from your local emergency management office.
    - Bring your pets indoors as soon as local authorities say trouble is on the way. Keep pets under your direct control; if you have to evacuate, you will not have to spend time trying to find them. Keep your dog on a leash.
    - If you have a room you can designate as a "safe room," put your emergency supplies in that room in advance, including your pet's crate and supplies. Have any medications and a supply of pet food and water inside watertight containers, along with your other emergency supplies. If there is an open fireplace, vent, pet door, or similar opening in the house, close it off with plastic sheeting and strong tape.
    - Listen to the radio periodically, and don't come out until you know it's safe.

6. **After the disaster**

    Your home may be a very different place after the emergency is over, and it may be hard for your pets to adjust.

    - Don't allow your pets to roam loose. Familiar landmarks and smells might be gone, and your pet will probably be disoriented. Pets can easily get lost in such situations.
    - While you assess the damage, keep dogs on leashes and cats

in carriers inside the house. If your house is damaged, your pets could escape.
- Be patient with your pets after a disaster. Try to get them back into their normal routines as soon as possible. Be ready for behavioral problems caused by the stress of the situation. If these problems persist, or if your pet seems to be having any health problems, talk to your veterinarian.
- If your community has been flooded, search your home and yard for wild animals who may have sought refuge there. Stressed wildlife can pose a threat to you and your pet.

7. **Be ready for everyday emergencies**

There may be times when you can't get home to take care of your pets. Icy roads may trap you at the office overnight, an accident may send you to the hospital—things happen. But you can make sure your pets get the care they need by making arrangements now:

Find a trusted neighbor, friend, or family member and give him or her a key to your house or barn. Make sure this back-up caretaker is comfortable and familiar with your pets (and vice versa).

Make sure your back-up caretaker knows your pets' whereabouts and habits.

8. **Plans aren't just for pets**

Disaster plans aren't only essential for the safety of pets. They should also be in place for family and friends. If you're responsible for other kinds of animals, such as horses, during natural disasters, disaster plans can be life-savers. Do not wait. Make your plan a priority.

CHAPTER 18
SAYING GOODBYE

This is a very difficult and emotional chapter for me to write as I have had to say goodbye to my six-year-old Saint Bernard, Sampson, who had died from bloat. Losing a beloved pet can be an enormous blow.

Psychology teaches us that there are seven stages of grief. However, this is not a fixed sequence of events; each individual experiences these stages in their own time and in their own way. To my mind, the greatest value of this model is to emphasize that grief is not one-dimensional. It manifests itself in a jumble of intense emotions. Dealing with grief is not a linear progression, but a fluid process with chaotic twists and turns. How these stages relate to each other has very little to do with logical thinking.

It is more accurate to think of grief as a series of frantic moves to re-orient yourself to the world after a big loss has left you emotionally off-balance (disoriented). You may want to keep this in mind as you read the following description of the well-known stages of grief.

Typically, the seven stages of grief are described as:
- Shock or disbelief
- Denial
- Anger
- Bargaining
- Guilt
- Depression
- Acceptance and hope

Again, these stages are not necessarily experienced by all individuals or in this particular order. Each individual's response to grief and loss is unique. Some of the stages may last for very little time, or for a long time, and they can recur; some individuals may not experience all of these stages.

SAYING GOODBYE

Typically, the first reaction to news of a loss is shock or disbelief, followed by denial. People will say things like "it's not true; it can't possibly happen to me; there must be a mistake; this kind of thing only happens to other people," etc. This may be your first reaction when you discover that your dog has been diagnosed with a fatal disease or has been injured so seriously that recovery is not possible.

Facing the reality of death often leads people to feel very angry and resentful. They may say things such as "This is so unfair." Guilt, on the other hand, is a way of making sense of what is happening, of regaining some form of control over the uncontrollable. You may begin to ask yourself what you could have done differently and to express feelings such as "It must be my fault."

Once the reality of death sets in, those grieving the loss feel overwhelmed and may become depressed. They may feel as if resistance to these feelings is futile. Anger, unrealistic bargaining, and depression represent a struggle against problems in the outside world, but also against our own inner demons.

I have spent time with people who are dying, and they eventually reach a stage in which they are fully aware of their impending death, but are neither angry nor depressed. They have found acceptance. Acceptance is about using the lessons we have learned in life to come to terms with the realities of the world, on our own terms. With acceptance comes hope.

The hard part for most of us is actually getting to this acceptance and hope. Most people go through this process with the help of friends and family. If you do not have a strong support system and are having a difficult time with the loss of a pet, know that help is available. Please take advantage of one of the following resources:

- The American Society for the Prevention of Cruelty to Animals' (ASPCA) Pet Loss Hotline: 800-946-4646. Enter pin number 140-7211 and then add your own phone number. An

- ASPCA counselor will contact you.
- The Association of Pet Loss and Bereavement: www.aplb.org.
- You can also check with local veterinary schools for information on local support groups.

Euthanasia

I am speaking from personal experience when it comes to having to make the decision to use euthanasia. When your gut tells you it's time, talk to your veterinarian about the appropriate next step. Many times, euthanasia is the only humane option.

In this procedure, your veterinarian will give your dog an overdose of anesthesia or barbiturate that will relax him and bring about a quick and painless death goodbye. As with many items in my book, the best advice I can give you is to be informed. Ask your veterinarian about the best time of day to do this. If you make your appointment for a time when the clinic is not busy—usually during the first appointment in the morning or the last one at night—they will be able to provide you with more privacy during this difficult time. You may also be able to arrange for the veterinarian to come to your house to do the procedure.

You will also have to choose whether you want to be present for the procedure. Keep in mind that it might upset your dog to see you extremely distraught. For myself, I felt it was the right thing to do for me to be there. But I will always remember going home with only my beloved dog's leash.

You will also have to decide what to do with your dog's remains. Your dog can be cremated with other animals or cremated individually, in which case her ashes can be returned to you. You may choose to bury your dog in a pet cemetery or, if permitted by local zoning laws, in your backyard.

CHAPTER 19
CONCLUSION

I know this sounds funny but I always tell my students, "I hope that you never have to use anything you have learned in this class." I will then pause, and with a serious expression I'll look around the room and then ask them, "Are you ready? Are you ready to provide first aid to your dog in the event of an emergency? Are you ready to have a first-aid kit on hand? Are you ready to take the time to muzzle for your safety? Are you ready to give your dog the gift of comfort?

Lastly, are you happy that you are prepared?" I am deeply moved when people thank me with deep sincerity for the information they have learned, and at times will even offer a hug.

After reading *K9 Medic*, I truly hope you have a good knowledge base on providing K9 first aid. Please keep in mind your safety and I encourage you to read this book several times and take the time to practice the skills in a non-emergency situation. I also encourage you to build a first-name relationship with your veterinarian and be a part of a special breed group of your choice. I hope that you find comfort in knowing that you are now better prepared and are able to handle any emergency involving your dog. I know many of you will truly make a difference.

If you would like to take the online class of this book you can find information at www.K9firstaidandCPR.com

I once heard that if you're lucky, you will have one really great dog in your life. On one hand I beg to differ, and think that each dog will bring his or her own set of unique bonding characteristics. Techniques that will render your heart venerable to deep love, and great pain in times of loss. On the other hand, I do reserve special place in my heart for my late Saint Bernard, Sampson. I lost Sampson to bloat in 2002 and find myself saddened by the emptiness he left behind. Yes, I still have his barrel that hung from his neck, and a box full of toys half torn up. Perhaps there will be a time I will part with these items but for now they offer a bit of comfort.

What I can tell you about dogs is we call them our best friends; you may very well like them more than you like people. You may have more photos of your dog than you do of your kids. You perhaps will even call them your kids. You hug them in a way that is special just to them. You make

CONCLUSION

funny sounds and voices as you open your heart to them. You will build them doghouses fit for a king. You will spend money you do not have in hopes to make them healthy. You will develop a bond like no other. You will never regret any time you spend with them.

Life is short, my friends. More importantly, our life on earth is precious time. Do not ignore its value; do not squander it in trivial pursuits; do not let it slip away and leave you unprepared. Life goes by so very fast. In closing, I wanted to share with you a K9 medic version of All I Really Need to Know:

K9 MEDIC

All I Really Need To Know
I Learned In K9 First Aid and CPR class.

Most of what I really need to know about how to live, and what to do, and how to be, I learned in K9 first aid and CPR class.

Share everything, even my slobbery ball.

Play fair and do not sit on the baby.

Don't bite people.

Put things back where you found them and do not bury them.

Try not to make a mess.

Don't eat things that aren't yours.

Licking is a form of affection.

Lick your paws before you eat.

Potty outside.

Warm cookies and cold milk are good for you, but not for me.

Live a balanced life—Eat, sleep, play.

Cuddle every day.

Take a nap every afternoon.

When you go out into the world, watch out for traffic.

Put me on a leash and stick together.

Be aware of wonder.

Love to the deepest depths of your heart.

INDEX

A

abrasions, 69
abscesses, 77
"All I Really Need to Know" (poem), 154
allergic reactions
    and anaphylactic shock, 54
    and insect bites, 73
    medication, 4
    and seizures, 85
    and snake bites, 131
animal bites, 62–64
antihistamine dosages, 73–74
appetite, poor, 77, 110, 113, 135
approaching an injured dog, 16–18
artificial respiration, 33–36

B

back, broken, 96
balance, loss of, 85, 109–110
bandages
    head, 77–79
    pressure, 65–66
    tail, 74–76
bee stings, 72–74
Benadryl (diphenhydramine), 4, 128
    dosage, 73–74
bite from injured dog
    avoiding, 17–18
    muzzling, 20–29
    restraining, 19–20

bites
    warning signs, 18
    animal, 62–64
    insect, 72–74
    wounds from, 76–77

bleeding
    controlling, 64–69
    ears, 77–79
    heavy, 61
    nosebleeds, 138
    pressure bandages, 65–66
    tourniquets, 67–69

bloat, 98–107. *See also* poisons
    breeds most at risk, 102, 107
    preventing, 104–106
    symptoms, 102–103
    treatment to reduce risk, 106

bones, broken
    back or neck, 96
    legs, 61

bones, dislocated, 96–97
brain scans, 89
breathing. *See also* choking; CPR
    congestion, 110
    difficulty, 73, 103, 109, 117, 130–132, 136
    and muzzles, 23
    normal, 9
    reverse sneezing, 85
    wheezing, 110

burns, 70–72

C

car accidents, 132–134
cerebrospinal fluid (CSF) analysis, 88
chemicals that poison, 111–112, 114–115
chest compressions, 36–40
choking, 45–52

INDEX

       Heimlich maneuver, 47–52
            dogs 20 pounds or less, 48–49
            dogs over 20 pounds, 49–52
       identifying, 46–47
claw injuries, 139
coat, 110, 132
collapse
       and bloat, 103
       and choking, 47
       and heat stroke, 117
       and poison, 109, 113, 129, 131
coma, 112, 115, 117. *See also* consciousness, determining
congestion, 110
consciousness, determining, 38. *See also* seizures
constipation, 110
convulsions. *See* seizures
coughing
       and bloat, 103
       and choking, 46
       and electric shock, 136
       and smoke inhalation, 132
       and vomiting, 23
CPR, 30–44
       artificial respiration, 33–36
       chest compressions, 36–40
           dogs less than 20 pounds, 40
           dogs over 20 pounds, 38–40
       method
           dogs 10 pounds or less, 42
           dogs more than 10 pounds, 42–43
       plans, 31–32
       when it fails, 43
CT (computerized tomography) scans, 89

D

death, 147–150
       euthanasia, 150

       grieving, 147–150
       support groups, 149–150
dehydration, 128
diarrhea
       and dehydration, 128
       and heat stroke, 117
       and poison, 110–114, 129
       and vomiting, 126–128
diphenhydramine, 4, 128
       dosage, 73–74
disaster planning, 140–146
       kit contents, 141–142
dislocated bones, 96–97
dizziness, 85, 109–110. *See also* seizures
dogfights, 76–77
drowning, 136

E

ear bleeding, 77–79
ear medications, 122
EEG (electroencephalogram), 88–89
elbows, dislocated, 96–97
electric shock, 136–137
Elizabethan collars (E-collars), 124
embedded objects, 76
emergencies, identifying, 7–15
       appearance, 8–9
       assessment triangle, 8–13
       breathing, 9
       circulation, 9–13
       pulse taking, 10–11
       temperature taking, 14–15
epilepsy, 83
euthanasia, 150
eyes
       blind appearance, 84
       bulging, 47

INDEX

eyewash, 6
glazed over, 84
healthy tissue, 13
injuries, 138–139
medications, 122
popping out of sockets, 29
tearing or discharge, 131–132, 135

F

fainting, 38, 109. *See also* seizures
fever, 63, 77, 128, 129
first-aid kits, 1–6
    contents of, 4–6
fishhook injuries, 137–138
food rationing, 126–127
foods that poison, 112–114
fractures, 91–97
    identifying, 92
    treating, 92–95
frostbite, 119–120
fur, 110, 132

G

gastric dilatation volvulus (GDV). *See* bloat
gastropexy, 106
glucose, 53–54
grieving, 147–150
gum tissue
    and bloat, 103
    healthy, 12–14
    and poison, 109, 114
    and shock, 55–56
    and smoke inhalation, 132
    ulcers, 137

H

head bandages, 77–79

heart rate
    elevated, 54–55, 103, 112–114, 117
    measuring, 9–11
heat stroke, 116–119
    symptoms, 117
    treatment, 118–119
Heimlich maneuver, 47–52
    dogs 20 pounds or less, 48–49
    dogs over 20 pounds, 49–52
hips, dislocated, 96–97

I

inflammatory bowel disease, 126
insect bites, 72–74
internal injuries, 61

J

jellyfish stings, 128

L

lacerations, 70
legs, broken, 61
lethargy, 77, 110, 114, 128
limping, 92, 134

M

medications, administering, 121–124
    Benadryl (diphenhydramine), 73–74
    ear, 122
    eye, 122
    liquid, 123
    ointments and creams, 124
    pills and capsules, 123–124
medications that poison, 111–112, 114
mouth ulcers, 137
MRI (magnetic resonance imaging), 89
mucus membranes, checking, 12–13

INDEX

muzzling an injured dog, 20–29
    making a muzzle, 23–26
    purchasing a muzzle, 26–28
    using a towel as a muzzle, 28–29

N

nasal discharge, 110
neck, broken, 96
nosebleeds, 138

O

ointments and creams, 124
oxygen, 53–54

P

pad wounds, 80–82
poisons, 108–115
    automotive products, 115
    caffeine, 112–113
    caustic substances, 111
    chemicals, 111–112
    chives, 114
    chocolate, 112
    garlic, 114
    grapes, 113
    household products, 114
    insecticides, 112
    lawn and garden products, 115
    macadamia nuts, 114
    medications for humans, 111–112
    onions, 114
    plants, 115
    raisins, 113
    rodenticides, 114
    symptoms, 109–110
    toads, 128–129
    what to do, 109

Xylitol, 113
porcupines, 134–135
pulse, taking, 10–11. *See also* heart rate

R

rabies, 62–64
    preventing, 64
    symptoms, 62–63
    treatment for, 63–64
restraining an injured dog, 19–20
reverse sneezing, 85

S

salivation, excessive, 110, 117, 129
scene safety, 16–17
scorpions, 131–132
scratching, 110
seizures, 83–90. *See also* poisons
    causes, 86–87
    diagnosing, 87–89
    identifying, 84–85
    what to do, 90
shivering, 55
shock, 53–57
    identifying, 54–56
    stages, 54
    treating, 56–57
skunks, 135
sleep behavior, 85
smoke inhalation, 132
snakebites, 129–131
    identifying snakes, 129–130
    symptoms, 130–131
    treatment, 131
sneezing, reverse, 85
splints, 92–94
sprains and strains, 91–97

INDEX

       identifying, 92
       treating, 92–95
status epilepticus, 89
stethoscope, using, 9–10
stomach ailments. *See* bloat; poisons; vomiting
support groups, 149–150

T

tail swelling and injuries, 74–76
teeth clenching, 84
thirst, excessive, 110
toads, 128–129
toenail injuries, 139
tongue ulcers, 137
tourniquets, 67–69

U

ulcers in the mouth, 137

V

vomiting, 125–128
    and bloat, 102–103
    causes, 126
    and choking, 47
    and heat stroke, 117
    inducing, 5
    and muzzles, 23
    and poison, 110, 112–114, 129
    and toads, 129
    treatment, 126–128

W

water rationing, 126–127
wheezing, 110
wild animal encounters, 134–135
wounds
    abrasions, 69

K9 MEDIC

bites, 62–64, 72–74, 76–77
bleeding control, 64–69
bones, 61
burns, 70–72
ears, 77–79
embedded objects, 76
fishhook injuries, 137–138
internal, 61
lacerations, 70
pads, 80–82
tails, 74–76
treatment basics, 59–61

ABOUT THE AUTHOR

ERIC ROTH was born and raised in Colorado. As a young man, he followed his childhood dream of becoming a firefighter, only to abandon the idea for a series of high-paying sales jobs. Life took an unexpected turn with the tragic loss of his father. This event inspired Roth to once again pursue his dreams. He was hired as a paramedic for a large city fire department in 2003. He immediately established himself as a well-respected educator, teaching CPR, first aid, advanced cardiac care, and pediatric life support.

Roth started his own company in 2010 in order to make the most of his teaching abilities. Although his business started out teaching human CPR, in a strange twist of fate his training branched into the canine world. Roth had discovered an educational void that left dog owners without vital knowledge. Canine first aid and CPR were born. Roth developed a paramedic-based canine CPR class, and has taught over eight hundred dog lovers since that time. Since there is no 911 for dogs, Roth's intention has been to fill that gap.

Roth continues to work as a 911 paramedic and is developing an online version of his traditional canine first aid and CPR classes. Roth is also working on a national program to help train and educate law enforcement and military personnel to provide canine first aid and CPR in the field.